THINKING THROUGH HISTORY

Peter Fisher
University of Newcastle

with

Ian Wilkinson
St Thomas More R C High School

and

David Leat
Series Editor

The *Thinking Through History* Team

Joanne Bush	Blyth Community High School, Northumberland
Anne de A'Echevarria	Lycée International de St-Germain-en-Laye, France
Alison Gray	Seaton Burn Community College, North Tyneside
Michael Hawthorn	Kenton Comprehensive School, Newcastle
Claire Harbottle	Transforming Key Stage 3 Consultant, Gateshead LEA
Patricia Hopkins	St Thomas More R C High School, North Tyneside
David Leat	University of Newcastle
Dawn Marshall	Washington High School, Sunderland
Samantha Martin	St Joseph's R C Comprehensive School, South Tyneside
Clare Peatfield	Prudhoe Community High School, Northumberland
Roger Purdy	St Bede's Catholic Comprehensive School, Co Durham
Anna Rossiter	Hexham Middle School, Northumberland
Claire Rogers	St Thomas More R C High School, North Tyneside
Sarah Robinson	St Edmund Arrowsmith R C High School, Wigan
Christine Straker	St Cuthbert's R C Comprehensive School, Newcastle
Ian Wilkinson	St Thomas More R C High School, North Tyneside

With additional help from

Sally Taverner	University of Newcastle

Contents

Thinking Through History

Thinking Through History

1 Thinking Through History

Introduction

This book is written *for* teachers who have an ambition. It was certainly written *by* teachers with an ambition – that pupils should be challenged to think, as they enjoy this different approach to history and learn from it. When pupils enjoy lessons and learning, it is certain that their teachers will also enjoy and learn. One of the downsides of the educational revolution since the introduction of the National Curriculum (NC) is that enjoyment has become a scarcer commodity. Teaching and learning should be fun! (although this 'fun' should be surrounded by 'rigour', which is true to both the nature of subject and to the profession of teaching young people to learn.)

The appearance of this teacher resource *Thinking Through History* is timely in several ways. Firstly, its range of Strategies offers ample opportunity 'to do things differently' through a combination of fun, challenge, motivation and rigour. Secondly, the series of changes in recent years affecting the organisation and perception of 11-18 education offers, in different ways, a window of opportunity for the teaching profession to step off the 'treadmill of syllabus coverage'.

In the meantime schools continue to be very pressurised places. The Government's top agenda item is raising standards. Indeed, improving literacy standards is a goal to which everyone would wish to aspire. However, it is less certain that more testing, performance monitoring, and improved National Curriculum and GCSE results necessarily means raised standards. There is a certain inevitability that exam results generally follow an upward trend as teachers learn how to prepare pupils more effectively for tests and exams. Teachers do teach to tests, and who can blame them? Witness the growth – and sales – in examination syllabus specific textbooks, often written by Examination Board examiners. The Ofsted inspection framework adds to the sense of being under the spotlight of public accountability.

The driving force for much of the frenetic assessment activity in schools is target setting. The target negotiated with the Local Education Authority is frequently translated into numbers of pupils who are expected or required to get specific grades at GCSE in each subject. This, in turn, may be translated into a GCSE class list which states the expected grade for each pupil based on value added data. This expected grade is pursued through frequent tests to monitor the performance of pupils.

But, and it is a big BUT, equal amounts of energy and money are NOT being devoted to professional development to help teachers improve their teaching. This is a classic case of pressure without support.

However, there are some helpful signs. It is recognized, albeit sporadically, that the goals of education cannot be fully realised just through higher grades in public examinations. It is increasingly asserted that, in an information economy with rapidly changing technologies, continuous re-skilling for new jobs will be essential. Current educational practice centred on the mastery of fixed bodies of knowledge appears to be increasingly out of step with such needs.

National Curriculum History at Key Stage 3

As far as National Curriculum history is concerned, the need for adaptability and flexibility have been recognised in the Statutory Requirements. Although, at first sight, the six Areas of Study may appear virtually identical to the 1995 post-Dearing version, the reality is that a landscape of potential opportunities has been created.

Thus, history teachers have entered a millennium where they have an open invitation in their planning and teaching:

- to significantly reduce the amount of prescribed content;
- to experiment with the sequence of areas studied;
- to pursue ideas of creativity and greater flexibility.

Moreover, these invitations to 'do things differently' have been endorsed and positively encouraged by all the key educational players including the DfES, QCA, Ofsted, and HMI. So, whilst we retain the all important *how* to teach history, the NC changes at Key Stage 3

> The National Curriculum (NC) for Key Stage 3 introduced from September 2000 with the inclusion of thinking skills;
> The specifications for AS and A2 (as part of Curriculum 2000), with their emphasis upon modularised learning and the promotion of Key Skills introduced in September 2000;
> The continued development of GNVQ courses;
> The revised criteria for all GCSE subjects at 14 - 16;
> The increasing emphasis upon transferable skills and lifelong learning.

have made the *where? what? when?* and *who?* of the work more responsive than before to each individual teacher and to the history department's decision making processes.

In 1999 the Department for Education and Employment published a research review *From Thinking Skills to Thinking Classrooms: a review and evaluation of approaches for developing pupils' thinking.* Key conclusion 1 stated that:

> *Current attempts to teach thinking are part of a more general thrust in educational reform which emphasises quality of thinking, processes, and thinking skills as a means to raise educational standards and to prepare children and young people for lifelong learning. Raising standards requires that attention is directed not only on what is to be learned but on how children learn and how teachers intervene to achieve this.*

(McGuinness, 1999)

The key conclusions also emphasise that subject specific infusion approaches offer the chance to embed teaching thinking within the curriculum, rather than relying on 'bolt on' courses which can be dropped easily. History is identified as one of the subjects well placed to do this.

Furthermore, when the *National Curriculum Handbook for Secondary Teachers in England* appeared in late 1999 it contained for the first time a rationale for the curriculum which recognises the need to 'learn how to learn'. Three sections are highlighted here.

1. Key Skills

Key Skills are defined in terms of helping learners to improve their learning and performance in education, life and work. They are listed as:

- Communication;
- Application of number;
- Information technology;
- Working with others;
- Improving own learning and performance;
- Problem solving.

Four of these areas can be substantially boosted through infusing *teaching thinking* into history.

Communication includes skills in speaking and listening: the ability to listen, understand and respond to others; and to participate effectively in group discussion. Skills in reading and writing include the ability to reflect critically on what is read, and critical analysis of their own and others' writing.

Working with others includes the ability to contribute to small group and whole class discussion. All subjects are expected to provide opportunities to appreciate the experience of others and consider different perspectives, and to benefit from what others think, say and do.

Improving own learning and performance involves pupils reflecting on and critically evaluating their work and ways to improve their learning and performance. *'They need to be able to identify the purposes of learning, to reflect on the processes of learning, to assess progress in learning, to identify obstacles or problems in learning and to plan ways to improve learning.'*

Problem solving includes the skills of identifying and understanding a problem, planning ways to solve it, and monitoring progress and reviewing solutions in tackling it.

2. Thinking Skills

For the first time, the National Curriculum stresses a focus for pupils on '*knowing how*' as well as '*knowing what*' and '*learning how to learn*'. It lists five Thinking Skills which '*complement the Key Skills and are embedded in the National Curriculum*'.

Information-processing skills enable pupils to gather information and more importantly to sort, classify, sequence, compare and contrast, and to analyse part/whole relationships.

Reasoning skills enable pupils to give reasons for their opinions and decisions and to use precise language to explain what they think.

Enquiry skills enable pupils '*to ask relevant questions, to pose and define problems, to plan* *what to do and how to research, to predict outcomes and anticipate consequences, and to test conclusions and improve ideas'.*

Creative thinking skills enable pupils to generate ideas and apply imagination in the search for alternative solutions.

Evaluation skills enable pupils to evaluate information and develop informed criteria for judging their own and others' thinking and ideas.

It is so tempting to say 'we already do that', or 'that is what good practice in history teaching is all about anyway'. Certainly some do it more and better than others. However, nobody does it as well as it might be done. Everybody thinks, but that is not to say that we think as well as we might. There is enormous scope for development for us all.

3. Citizenship

In the words of the National Curriculum, citizenship promotes spiritual, moral, social and cultural development, and makes pupils more self confident and responsible in and out of the classroom. Whilst one might entertain some scepticism about moral panics that thrust citizenship higher up the agenda, there is a serious point about the way in which classrooms can prepare pupils to be decent human beings.

The programmes of study for KS3 citizenship include:

'Knowledge and understanding about becoming informed citizens.

Pupils should be taught about:

a. human rights and responsibilities;

b. the diversity of identities and the need for mutual respect and understanding;

g. the importance of resolving conflict fairly;

h. the significance of media.'

'Developing skills of enquiry and communication.

Pupils should be taught to:

a. think about topical political, spiritual, moral, social and cultural issues;

b. justify orally and in writing a personal opinion about such issues;

c. contribute to group and exploratory class discussions and take part in debates.'

'Developing skills of participation and responsible action.

Pupils should be taught to:

a. use their imagination to consider other people's experiences, and be able to think about, express and explain views that are not their own.'

There are some cross references to particular subjects, which include history, but without doubt a *teaching thinking* approach will make these aspirations a reality for pupils and avoid the need for citizenship lessons.

QCA Schemes of Work for Key Stage 3 NC History

QCA's suggested *Schemes of Work for KS3* (2000) illustrate the three features outlined above of Key Skills, Thinking Skills and Citizenship.

They also offer exemplification of the freedoms and opportunities to *'do things differently'* referred to earlier.

Amongst QCA's 22 Units are opportunities to build upon the different *Thinking Through History* Strategies presented in this book. This may be attempted at two levels.

Many history Units – through their objectives, activities and possible outcomes – can be matched against the Thinking Skills outlined within the NC, such as information-processing skills and enquiry skills. *The Teachers' Guide* provides some cross-references on page 16. (QCA, 2000)

There are two specific Units which infuse a *Thinking Through History* approach into the whole Unit of work. The first, Unit 19, adopts a depth study into the key question *'How and why did the Holocaust happen?'* Through medium and short term curriculum plans a variety of Thinking Skills strategies are presented as possible ways to unpack some of the stereotypes and issues surrounding this frequently taught topic at Key Stage 3 and GCSE. Unit 22 allows the total flexibility to study the *'role of any individual'* in the past *'and assess their impact – for good or ill'*. The key theme of the Unit offers an exploration of *'second-order'* historical concepts of *'change'*, *'significance'* and *'interpretation'* through a series of *Thinking Through History* Strategies.

This book, therefore, aims to help history teachers improve their practice, make lessons more stimulating and challenging for all concerned, and make pupils better learners. It is a book that connects theory and practice. These Strategies have been classroom tested and there is a body of theory that explains why they work and how they can be exploited to maximum value. The Strategies provide a huge stimulus for professional development. They create excitement, new ideas, some anxiety, the need to collaborate and to find out more about pupils' learning.

What is Teaching Thinking?

A lot of thinking already happens in classrooms. It is tempting for teachers to say 'we do that already' and there is an element of truth in that response. Taking the broader view, it is difficult to claim that there is enough attention explicitly focused on higher order *thinking* in British classrooms. If there were, classrooms would be quite different places. Pupils would ask more questions of an enquiring nature; teachers would not dominate the agenda; there would be more surprise and ambiguity, more motivation, less boredom, more connections to the world outside the classroom – and perhaps fewer tests.

Teaching thinking has to be defined partly by what it is *not*. It is *not* a didactic attempt to teach a defined set of thinking 'skills' which must then be practised. Rather, it is the creation of challenging learning experiences which call for high level thinking: information processing; reasoning; enquiry; creative thinking; and evaluation. The subject learning outcomes may be important. But of equal or greater value is the learning about reasoning and thinking, which demands that teachers begin to develop a vocabulary for pupils to use. Without words, thinking and learning are so hard to talk about.

Teaching thinking lessons tend to have the following characteristics:

- they contain challenging tasks that encourage pupils to use what they already know;
- there is seldom one single correct answer, and the teacher does not necessarily offer a best solution;
- work is highly co-operative – all tasks are initially done in groups with talk encouraged;
- the teacher only gives help when absolutely necessary, so that pupils have the chance to struggle;
- in plenary and debriefing there should be discussion both about solutions and how the task has been done;
- the teacher seeks to help pupils to make connections between the thinking and learning from the task and other contexts in order to build a bigger picture – **transfer**;
- teachers sometimes cannot predict the learning outcomes of a lesson, or respond to all the pupils' questions or comments;
- assessment is largely diagnostic and formative and much less summative, and listening to and watching groups is as important as marking work.

Thinking Through History, therefore, is also about professional development. Making these Strategies work effectively requires you to take risks, develop your practice and learn more about students' learning. (See *Chapter 10*.)

The Strategy Exemplars have been trialled and written up by fifteen classroom teachers: some experienced heads of department, others with a few years under their belts and one or two in their first years of teaching! All have a close connection with Newcastle University Department of Education, all being ex-PGCE students or experienced mentors in the Newcastle University teacher training partnership. These teachers teach in a wide variety of contexts: 9-13, 11-16, 11-18, 13-18, disadvantaged catchments, more favoured catchments, Roman Catholic schools, inner city areas, urban suburbs and old mining communities. Three of the teachers are teaching at a school awarded 'Training School' status. This all says a great deal about the potential for the Strategies for differentiation. It can also give you confidence that these strategies and materials DO WORK.

Levels of Use

This book can be used at four different Levels. The higher the Level, the greater the potential impact on students' learning. But also correlated with the higher Levels of use is an increased need to restructure practice – which costs time and effort.

Level 1. You use the photocopiable materials as they are to create more interesting and challenging lessons.

Level 2. All the Strategies are flexible and adaptable and can be used across a wide spectrum of ages and abilities. To demonstrate this, each Strategy is exemplified by three contexts that range in subject matter and age group. Many of the Exemplars can be used with equal success from Y7 to Y13 classes, with only the smallest of changes. They are fine examples of differentiation by outcome. We hope that most teachers will be able to use the templates and adapt the Strategies for other topics. All of the Strategies address the series of key concepts which underpin the study of history – be it at Key Stage 3, GCSE or above. Different Exemplars place emphasis upon developing *'knowledge, skills and understanding'*.

Level 3. To the above, one starts to add debriefing, through which pupils are encouraged to talk and think about their thinking. Two main lines of questioning are demanded for this: *'what is your answer/solution/outcome?'* with supplementary questions to encourage pupils to be explicit, as well as encouragement to other pupils to comment, chip in and question; and *'how did you tackle the problem? how did you do it?'* through which one gets pupils to talk about the processes they have used. Thinking and talking about thinking are termed **metacognition**. This is the process that starts pupils gaining an insight into thinking and learning, and building up an explicit understanding of reasoning patterns and mental models that can be **transferred** to other contexts. Debriefing is hard to do well, especially at first, and can have the effect of making you feel like a novice again. At this Level professional development becomes a significant issue. Some Exemplars contain descriptions of how these tasks were debriefed. Although these provide some helpful signposts, be prepared for the fact that debriefing is an advanced professional skill, which needs deliberate practice and development.

Level 4. Beyond Level 3, you are very definitely into the area of school policy relating to curriculum development and staff development. If you want to make *teaching thinking* fully effective this approach to teaching needs to be found beyond just one department or faculty. There need to be policies in the school development plan relating to assessment, professional development and an integrated whole-school approach to the curriculum. This is a tall order, but one which is being broached by a number of pioneering schools.

We have written this book primarily for those who are concerned with using the Strategies at Levels 1 and 2. The Strategies deal principally with these Levels, with some guidance on starting to address debriefing (Level 3). The sections on Professional Development and Curriculum Development in the last part of the book (pages 132-143) are aimed at those who wish to consider Levels 3 and 4 in more depth.

We make no apology for the appearance of some theory about learning and curriculum development. For too long teaching has drifted towards a utilitarian, delivery mentality. One of the dangers inherent in this is that it makes the profession very vulnerable to politicians, an imposed curriculum and Ofsted judgements. There are ambitions to make teaching an evidence and research based profession. This is some way off, but *teaching thinking* is a wonderful vehicle for teachers who wish to undertake action research, because it helps 'take the lid off' pupils' thinking and learning. We expect doctors to know a great deal about physiology, illness and treatments – teachers have to know how to get students to learn.

Big Concepts in History

Amongst any gathering of history teachers, you could predict that a large measure of agreement might exist concerning the 'overarching' or 'structural' concepts which underpin the nature of the discipline. This position has come about through teachers' experience at 'looking over the parapet' in their planning, teaching and assessment of the 'big concepts' which underpin the development of pupils' knowledge, understanding and skills.

This arises initially from the conceptually focused philosophy behind the highly influential Schools' Council History Project – introduced from the mid-1970s onwards. These 'New History' approaches emphasised that the nature of history can be explored through the study of its basic concepts:

evidence;

empathy;

cause;

change and continuity.

These concepts became enshrined into the Assessment Criteria for all the new GCSE history courses. Although the feasibility of assessing 'empathy' caused much 'angst', few doubted the desirability of promoting an awareness of past peoples' differing attitudes, values and beliefs.

In the past decade, the **big concepts** became further embedded in the Key Elements section of each successive version of the history National Curriculum and accompanying Attainment Targets and Level Descriptors. Within the five aspects of knowledge, skills and understanding the current version (2000) focuses upon:

'time/chronology – *when did it happen?*

range of ideas, attitudes and beliefs – *what did different people think?*

situation and diversity – *what was it like?*

change – *what changed?*

cause and effect – *why did it change? what was the result?*

continuity – *how long did it last?*

significance – *what was important and long-lasting?*

interpretations – *what are the differences between different accounts?*

sources – *what evidence is there?*

communication – *how convincing is this to a reader?*'

(Nichol, 1995)

All the Thinking Skills Strategies within this book were devised with the belief that an explicit focus upon **big concepts** is both necessary and desirable in developing pupils' historical understanding. Equally, notions of progression by 'revisiting' a limited number of 'overarching concepts' – applied with increasing sophistication to differing historical contexts – is embedded within the Exemplars.

By way of examples, the **Concept Maps** ask pupils to think about issues of *cause, effect and significance*. The **Mysteries** focus upon pupils arriving at a plausible *explanation* based upon manipulating *evidence*. By way of contrast, the **Reading Photographs** and **Community of Enquiry** Strategies offer fertile entry points in matters of differing *attitudes, values, cultures, morals, citizenship and historical interpretations*.

Progression

If you have any ambition to make *teaching thinking* a coherent thread in your history teaching then progression becomes an issue – but it is an issue in the subject anyway.

Christine Counsell (2000) provides an interesting commentary on the debate regarding progression, which we would recommend. Our general view is that progression has to be viewed very broadly in *teaching thinking*. As Christine points out, it is extremely difficult to disentangle the connections between substantive knowledge and second-order ideas. We do not believe that we can set out a progression in second-order concepts onto which you could map the Strategies in this book.

The Strategies should be regarded as providing rich learning experiences. The exact nature of that experience will vary considerably from class to class, as the outcomes will vary. Some of these materials can be used with both Y7 and adults. Both have fun and learn a lot, but the learning outcomes will be different. The teacher's job is one of diagnosing what pupils find difficult and then helping them to overcome the difficulty and move on. Sometimes this is collective frailty, such as a class that finds it difficult to listen to each other, and sometimes it will be an individual barrier, such as a pupil who does not know the meaning of a word. The Strategies are extremely powerful at helping you diagnose 'next steps'. Ask yourself '*What is Richard able to do that makes his response better than Paolo's?'* or *'What is it about Ameeta's reasoning that makes her answers more impressive?'* or *'What has this group done that has taken them so much further?'* Look for progression in so much more than historical understanding: look for progression in the ability and willingness to learn.

This is, potentially, a floppy and dissatisfying stance. People want answers. At present we don't have them. Tackling progression should be viewed as closely-allied to assessment. Most assessment should be about diagnosing what pupils can and cannot do, and then teaching so that they can improve. Progression needs to be less about following a prescribed route, and much more about drawing the map to know the lie of the land.

Using the Exemplars

Each Strategy is demonstrated through three Exemplars which were developed for and trialled with classes of different age and ability. This demonstrates the inherent flexibility of each Strategy, although the intentions and outcomes of using a particular Strategy will vary with the age and ability of the class. For example using a **Mystery** with a Y7 group is likely to contribute as much to intellectual development as it will to learning content. Using a **Mystery** with a sixth form group, however, may be focused more on developing skills that are important in decision-making and data response papers. However, you should not feel abashed if your intention is simply to make some lessons more challenging for the pupils and perhaps more interesting for you. This is really worth doing for its own sake.

The Style

This book is different. On the one hand it offers some tried and tested Strategies – classroom devised and trialled – which address current agendas. On the other hand it can be used as a catalyst for reflection on teaching, learning and your own professional development.

Fifteen teachers have collaborated to write this book. The Strategies have been edited to achieve a degree of conformity in coverage and style, but we decided not to make them all the same. This leaves room for individuality, as well as for the contribution of your own professional skill in planning and delivery. Some write ups give greater attention to launching, some to managing and others to debriefing. Not everything went smoothly with every trial – you should therefore not be too dismayed if your first experiences are not a brilliant success. You learn over time to make these Strategies work effectively. We hope, however, that we present descriptions of excitement, confusion, insight and real learning to convince you that this is history with a difference. The write ups of the trials are provided to give you some guidelines, to enable you to avoid predictable pitfalls, and to make you think seriously about the issues you will have to address with your classes. The Strategies are not exact templates to give you instant success. We provide some materials and scaffolding, but you still have to build the house.

In some Exemplars the writer describes what she/he did in the past tense. In others, the writer adopts a future tense. *'You should…'* is a sign that the writer has used the Strategy in a variety of contexts on numerous occasions and feels more certain about generalising advice. The former suggests less experience with the Strategy and therefore less certainty.

The Rationale is written as a general introduction to each Strategy, and gives a broad view of the value of the Strategy and/or the personal motivation of the teacher for using it. This is not to persuade you of the correctness of one view, but rather to help you think about the potential relevance and power of the Strategy as you watch the students engage with it and talk about it afterwards.

The following headings are used for each Exemplar:

The Context gives the background to the class and the topic that the Strategy was employed with. It gives some idea of the content that had gone before and some of the characteristics of the class. In most cases, however, matching the preceding content is not vital. But what has gone before can alter both the way the activity proceeds and the outcomes. So, for example, a **Lifeline** can be used at the end of a module to help pupils make connections between separate knowledge items and thus consolidate their understanding, but it could also be used at the beginning to stimulate a class and to raise questions which can form the core of an enquiry.

Precise behavioural objectives are not given because the activities do not generally fit a linear learning model and do not have simple behavioural outcomes that can be predetermined. It is very hard to say what pupils will learn; they are being provided with learning experiences and some of the purposes of the debriefing are to find out what they have learned, help them to identify it, give it a name and demonstrate its importance and relevance. Therefore we prefer to talk about *possible* learning outcomes. It does help preparation if you have some idea about what they might learn, but you also have to be on the lookout for the unexpected. However, this is not to imply that objectives cannot or should not be written for lessons using these materials, rather that their exact nature will depend upon the context within which you are teaching.

Preparation gives suggestions about what could/should be done before the lesson to make it run smoothly and to give you the maximum chance of success. This does not excuse you from planning the lesson in some detail. The Strategies and Exemplars are not worksheets or textbooks that can be dished out and used with no thought. They are not teacher-proof. We would expect some people to rewrite some of the materials, to better fit their particular context. When you take up something new and different you need to go back to square one and not take too much for granted. More specifically, you might need to:

- think about the launching;
- have a written note of what instructions you will give, and perhaps refer to it during the lesson;
- think about the managing of the activity, so that you support and encourage but don't interfere too much;
- plan the debriefing: allow time for it, know some of the questions you will ask, give some thought to how you will respond to anything pupils say;
- prepare some follow up work.

Launching. The first time that you use a Strategy with a class you may need to persuade them to accept the relevance and the different demands being made. This is especially the case if they are used to a diet of undemanding lessons with correct answers. These activities can make students feel threatened because they are unfamiliar. We have used the word *launching* to establish a particular analogy. A boat is stationary on a slipway. The chocks/brakes are removed, you give it a shove, and it gathers momentum down the slipway. You are giving the students a shove and they gather speed, because at heart thinking is something natural which we do enjoy (unless we have learned to steer clear of it). The boat enters the water, a new medium, and with a bit of luck it floats freely and independently. The students start to think for themselves as they do the task. The debriefing process can be likened to the boat being fitted out so that it is thoroughly seaworthy with all its equipment and trained crew (thinking resources and strategies – students become independent learners!). As you will appreciate, this does not happen in one lesson, and you have to launch the boat over and over again. You will notice that in some write ups, where classes had been exposed to the Strategy or others before, launching was less of an issue because the boat was already floating.

Instructions. These will help you avoid a few of the pitfalls, but of course they are not all given to the pupils in one big slab. Some of the instructions were committed to paper in the trials, in which case these sheets are included, but in other cases they were done verbally.

Managing the activity. Perhaps the single most useful piece of advice here is to think about your intentions for each particular activity. To some extent you will be concerned with the learning of content, because the activities are not content free. Therefore you will have some regard to this. But overall, your paramount concern should be with developing the students as learners. If you interfere unnecessarily or too much you will stunt their growth. If you leave them stranded they won't make any progress and they will get frustrated. This uneasy middle point has been termed contingent teaching – providing just enough support to encourage pupils to engage and learn but not too much that they use you as a crutch and learn nothing. (Another term used in similar contexts is **scaffolding.**) We all have to forgive ourselves for getting this wrong at times. Nonetheless each Strategy contains useful practical advice about making it work well.

Debriefing. This is the very hardest part to get right when *teaching thinking*. At the same

The Exemplars

Strategy	Key Skills	Thinking Skills	QCA KS3 Unit	Topic
Odd One Out Exemplar 1: The Battle of Hastings Y7	Communication Working with others Improving own learning and performance Problem solving	IP, R, CT, Ev	2	Medieval Monarchs
Odd One Out Exemplar 2: Plains Indians Y8	Communication Working with others Improving own learning and performance Problem solving	IP, R, CT, Ev	–	The Indigenous Peoples of North America
Odd One Out Exemplar 3: Trench Warfare Y9	Communication Working with others Improving own learning and performance Problem solving	IP, R, CT, Ev	18	Twentieth Century Conflicts
Concept Maps Exemplar 1: The Abolition of Slavery Y9	Communication Working with others Improving own learning and performance Problem solving	IP, R, En, CT, Ev	15	Black Peoples of America
Concept Maps Exemplar 2: Why did the Japanese bomb Pearl Harbour? Y9/Y10	Communication Working with others Improving own learning and performance Problem solving	IP, R, En, CT, Ev	18	Twentieth Century Conflicts
Lifelines Exemplar 1: The Peasants' Revolt Y7	Communication Application of number Working with others Improving own learning and performance	IP, R, En, CT	2 3	Medieval Monarchs Medieval People
Lifelines Exemplar 2: Germ Y9/Y10	Communication Application of number Working with others Improving own learning and performance	IP, R, En, CT	20 21	Twentieth Century Scientific Discoveries
Lifelines Exemplar 3: The Rise of Hitler Y9/Y10/Y11	Communication Application of number Working with others Improving own learning and performance	IP, R, En, CT	18 19 22	Twentieth Century Conflicts Holocaust Role of Individual
Mysteries Exemplar 1: Runaways Y8/Y9	Communication Working with others Improving own learning and performance Problem solving	IP, R, En, CT, Ev	11	Industrial Changes
Mysteries Exemplar 2: Pit Disaster! Y8/Y9/Y10	Communication Working with others Improving own learning and performance Problem solving	IP, R, En, CT, Ev	11	Industrial Changes
Mysteries Exemplar 3: Wilf's War Y9	Communication Working with others Improving own learning and performance Problem solving	IP, R, En, CT, Ev	18 22	Twentieth Century Conflicts Role of Individual
Reading Photographs and Pictures Exemplar 1: Jews in Germany Y9	Improving own learning and performance Problem solving	En, CT, Ev	19 22	Holocaust Role of Individual
Reading Photographs and Pictures Exemplar 2: The Home Front Y9-Y12	Improving own learning and performance Problem solving	En, CT, Ev	7 18	Images Twentieth Century Conflicts

Strategy	Key Skills	Thinking Skills	QCA KS3 Unit	Topic
Pictures from Memory Exemplar 1: Medieval Life Y7	Communication Working with others	IP, R	3	Medieval People
Pictures from Memory Exemplar 2: Motte and Bailey Castle Y7	Communication Working with others	IP, R	2	Medieval Monarchs
Story-telling Exemplar 1: The Spanish Armada Y7/Y8	Communication Working with others Improving own learning and performance	IP, R, En, CT, Ev	5	Elizabeth 1
Story-telling Exemplar 2: The Atomic Bomb Y9	Communication Working with others Improving own learning and performance	IP, R, En, CT, Ev	18 21	Twentieth Century Conflicts Scientific Discoveries
Story-telling Exemplar 3: The Hundred Days Y12	Communication Working with others Improving own learning and performance	IP, R, En, CT, Ev	–	–
Community of Enquiry: **Philosophy through History** Exemplar 1: A Border Conflict Y8	Communication Working with others Improving own learning and performance Problem solving	IP, R, En, CT, Ev	8	The Civil Wars
Community of Enquiry: **Philosophy through History** Exemplar 2: 38 Witnesses Y9	Communication Working with others Improving own learning and performance Problem solving	IP, R, En, CT, Ev	19 22	Holocaust Role of Individual
Community of Enquiry: **Philosophy through History** Exemplar 3: Circles Y8/Y9	Communication Working with others Improving own learning and performance Problem solving	IP, R, En, CT, Ev	–	The Indigenous Peoples of North America

NC Thinking Skills

IP = Information Processing

R = Reasoning

En = Enquiry

CT = Creative Thinking

Ev = Evaluation

Links to the KS3 NC Citizenship requirements	
Story-telling Exemplar 1: The Spanish Armada **Story-telling** Exemplar 2: The Atomic Bomb	Pupils represent a key issue of global conflict, involving consideration of the moral and scientific interface. Issues of conflict resolution may well arise.
Story-telling Exemplar 3: The Hundred Days	Pupils will evaluate the role of an individual and the importance of resolving conflict fairly.
Community of Enquiry: **Philosophy through History** Exemplar 1: A Border Conflict	Pupils consider other peoples' experiences and find out about legal and human rights, religious and regional diversity, and the importance of resolving conflict.
Community of Enquiry: **Philosophy through History** Exemplar 2: 38 Witnesses	Pupils investigate a key issue of an individual's rights and responsibilities. Pupils apply understanding to suggest tentative explanations of why the vast majority of people allowed the Nazi persecution of minorities to take place.
Community of Enquiry: **Philosophy through History** Exemplar 3: Circles	Pupils enquire into the origins of the culture clash which arose because of the differing value systems of the peoples living in the American West.

time it is the most crucial because it helps determine whether you have had just an interesting and challenging lesson (good in itself) or whether you have really gone further and helped the pupils consolidate the learning and transfer it to other contexts – the multiplier factor.

Not all of the Exemplars have details about debriefing. The teacher may have felt that it was not appropriate, or because circumstances – such as time – ruled it out. For our purposes here it is useful to talk about four possible strands to debriefing:

- to get pupils to explain their answer/solution at length;
- to ask pupils about their mental processes as they did a task or tackled a problem;
- to ask them about the patterns in reasoning that they employed; (this may emerge in discussion). These constitute **thinking about thinking** or **metacognition**.
- to draw their attention to other contexts where the same reasoning is valuable. These may be in other topics in history, in other subjects, or in their everyday lives. This is termed **bridging** and the intention is to get them to **transfer** their learning from the history lesson to the other contexts.

All the contributors to this book find debriefing a difficult practice to establish for a variety of reasons, some of which are logistical (such as fitting it into a packed lesson), and some of which are intellectual(it is hard for pupils to engage with). Ambitions in relation to debriefing are therefore cautious. We hope to be able to get you to do some. Make a start at least!

Links to the NC Citizenship Requirements

In terms of their content, virtually all the *Thinking Through History* Exemplars explore the significant overlaps between history and citizenship. Significantly, they do so in such a way that the dimensions of developing an understanding of citizenship are subfused within the historical topic(as Wrenn, 1999, has argued) rather than simply be 'bolted-on' as a spurious attempt to 'add value' to the history curriculum.

The table on page 11 illustrates how two of the *Thinking Through History* Strategies and their Exemplars have direct links to the KS3 (and KS4) Citizenship requirements.

More importantly though, the very process of conducting *thinking skills* Strategies in the classroom can often act as a powerful 'model' of participation in learning for pupils. All the Strategies encourage co-operation, communication and reasoned conciliation. Within the book certain Strategies and Exemplars are designed to confront – explicitly – aspects of the relationships, tensions and dilemmas faced by historical people, caught up in the uncertainty of events and themes. Some of these can be used as a springboard to explore the wider implications and issues affecting people in past and present societies.

Odd One Out

2 Odd One Out

Rationale

Many games make an excellent framework for *thinking* strategies. After all, games are mostly enjoyable and they make you think a bit. Alastair Smith, writing about accelerated learning (1996) makes the point that a high challenge/low stress environment is best for learning. It is worth reflecting on the number of important skills that are employed in playing *Monopoly* well, to say nothing of *Bridge*. **Odd One Out** draws on the heritage of good games, by getting students to think about the characteristics of things.

Unless you can identify the most important characteristics of a phenomenon then you can't classify it and can't describe it well, or associate it with other important related information. This skill is **classification**.

The **Odd One Out** Strategy uses a simple format in asking students to pick the 'Odd One Out' from a list of words – although as you will see there are a number of variations on this basic theme. The Strategy can be used at the beginning of a topic, as a starting point, to see what students already know, or perhaps more effectively, as an end point to assess and revise a unit.

The advantages and strengths may be summarised as follows:

- Students become more familiar with the meanings of key vocabulary, related to the characteristics that help pick the 'Odd One Out', eg social, economic, political, or cultural factors. This heightened awareness is very important during revision so that students understand key command words in public examination questions.
- Students are encouraged to see the similarities and differences between key terms, rather than seeing them as a collection of disconnected words. As a result students may acquire a grasp of the 'bigger picture', which sets the internal structure of the topic in its wider context (Riley, 1999). In this manner, **Concept Maps** may be deployed to provide a rapid, yet rigorous overview of historical topics. (Riley, 1999)
- The characteristics of a historical concept such as 'change' may be considered, eg factors, reasons, motives, causes, effects, consequences, implications, significance.
- The essential similarities – and differences – of events can be made into a point of focus, often through discussion of appropriate and inappropriate historical terminology, eg why is one event described as a 'riot', whilst another one carries the status of a 'revolt'? What key differences are there between a 'rebellion' and a 'revolution'?
- **Odd One Out** is good fun and makes the teacher think as much as the pupils.
- The Strategy can be done quickly, in as little as 10-15 minutes, and in a variety of groupings, which makes it very flexible. Use it as an extension task for fast finishers, a paired task as one activity in a lesson, or as a whole lesson activity.
- As it is fairly easy to make **Odd One Out** work, it is really interesting to go round and listen to students: you get a 'window' into how they think.
- It is an easy Strategy to explain to other members of staff.

Thinking Skills

Information-processing skills enable pupils to gather information and more importantly to sort, classify, sequence, compare and contrast, and to analyse part-whole relationships.

Reasoning skills enable pupils to give reasons for their opinions and decisions and to use precise language to explain what they think.

Evaluation skills enable pupils to evaluate information and develop informed criteria for judging their own and others' thinking and ideas.

The ability to classify is a central attribute, because the mastery of all other concepts rests upon it.

Having a secure vocabulary in the subject is both required at KS3 and vital to 14-19 examination performance.

Odd One's Out may expose pupils to the difficult 'semi-technical' nature of much historical language.

Nuances of meaning, such as these examples, can aid pupils' understanding of how peoples' actions have been explained.

Being able to listen to students is vital to successful debriefing.

The Battle of Hastings

Context

This activity was taught to a very low ability Year 7 group – many of whom had Statements of Special Educational Needs – at the end of a topic on the Battle of Hastings. The group was generally a noisy, lively group that took a long time to settle down to work. Many of the group have severe learning difficulties, one has emotional and behavioural development (EBD) problems.

Within this topic pupils had previously studied:

- the situation in England leading up to the battle;
- about Edward the Confessor dying without leaving an heir;
- why there were three claimants to the throne;
- Godwinson's defeat of Hardraada;
- Duke William's preparation for the battle.

The learning outcomes of the activity were:

- to consolidate pupils' existing knowledge and understanding of the topic;
- to indicate the level of understanding of the pupils which, in turn, might lead to some revealing information for diagnostic assessment purposes.

Preparation

Very little preparation was needed other than the time to compile the wordlists, sets, instruction sheets and to photocopy. In this respect it was no different to preparing a worksheet for a 'usual' lesson. I did find that anticipating pupils' answers before the lesson proved to be beneficial.

> Throughout the book you are encouraged to use your professional judgement, but this should not result in taking the challenge out of the activities.

Launching

Pupils were informed that there were going to 'play a game' of 'Odd One Out'. The use of the words 'play a game' was important. Clearly the class were taken with the idea of 'playing a game' and adopted a different outlook to the lesson. 'They' were going to 'play' – not my usual 'today we are going to learn about …'. It was 'playing' not 'learning', to them.

> This may be viewed as an example of **bridging**, which can help pupils see a more general relevance.to the activity.

The class were given a brief explanation of how to play the game, with two examples on the board:

Question 'Which is the 'Odd One Out' from apple, banana, cabbage, orange?'

Answer: 'Cabbage, is the 'Odd One Out'. It is a vegetable, the others are fruits.'

Question: 'Which is the 'Odd One Out' from car, bus, taxi, train?'

Answer: 'Train, because whilst all are forms of transport, train routes can only go where track exists … so trains are less flexible.'

We had a brief 5-minute brainstorming session of key historical words that we had recently used during the 1066 topic. With some prompting the pupils came up with a good selection of words, which were arranged in a spider diagram on the board.

Instructions

1 Give out the **Word List** (this will vary from the spider diagram on the board) and an **Instruction Sheet** to pairs of pupils (see *Resources 1-3*). Ask them to read through quickly.

2 Read through **Task 1**. Explain that the Sets and numbers refer to words on the **Word List**. Everyone should be able to see both the **Instructions** and the **Word List**.

3 Explain that each Set of words has an 'Odd One Out'. They have to decide which is the 'Odd One Out' and explain why. Stress the importance of explaining why their word is – in their view – the 'Odd One Out'. What is it about the two or three other words which makes them similar? What is it about the 'Odd One Out' word which makes it so different?

4 Emphasise the importance of discussing and agreeing in pairs *before writing anything down*, as either partner must be able to explain their answer. Tell the pupils to write down their answers and – briefly – their reason *why?*

Managing the activity

This was relatively easy. One or two pupils needed further explanation and guidance. But once the pupils got the idea, they tackled the work with enthusiasm. Apart from my initial teacher-talk to explain the activity, I spent most of the lesson monitoring in the background and was intrigued at the pupil-paired discussions of their 'Odd Ones Out'. Occasionally I was asked to help and advise the pupils on how to form their reasons for a certain word being the 'Odd One Out'. A number of pupils in this lower ability class reached Task 3, which involves making their own Sets and 'Odd Ones Out'. The majority got on to Task 2 by adding one extra word onto the Set from Task 1.

However since the whole point of the Strategy is to provide pupils with opportunities to characterise, classify and justify then it is not simply a matter of 'coverage', but rather the 'learning journey' that is important.

Debriefing

This was short, and involved pupils going over their reasons for their choice of the 'Odd One Out'. It was also an ideal opportunity to clear up any misunderstandings of events or of the words and their meanings that the pupils' responses revealed.

Evaluation

Overall, I found **Odd One Out** to be a good activity to use in the classroom. The class enjoyed the lesson, as it was a change from the usual teacher-led lesson. From a teaching point of view it was enjoyable, since it demanded a different style from me: for larger parts of the lesson I was in the background, only giving help when needed. Although the class was learning whilst 'playing', importantly, they were also learning from their peers. Overall I was more than happy with the responses from this class of lower ability pupils.

This is just one example of many of the vital role of talk in aiding understanding.

Teaching thinking emphasises the learning process as well as the learning outcomes.

This is one example of how *teaching thinking* can aid differentiation by outcome.

Word List

1. Harold Godwinson	19. invade
2. shield	20. King Edward the Confessor
3. England	21. Pevensey
4. archers	22. foot-soldier
5. fleet	23. tactic
6. forest	24. Hastings
7. died	25. knights
8. army	26. retreat
9. wind	27. Normandy
10. Norway	28. spear
11. Duke William	29. south
12. Battle of Stamford Bridge	30. coast
13. march	31. hill
14. London	32. Harald Hardraada
15. exhausted	33. throne
16. north	34. troops
17. battle	35. sail
18. France	36. arrow
	37. bullet

Resource 2   **Word List – Sets of Words**

Set A	**1**	**11**	**30**	**32**
Set B	**3**	**10**	**16**	**24**
Set C	**20**	**19**	**7**	**33**
Set D	**4**	**27**	**22**	**34**
Set E	**5**	**18**	**8**	**35**
Set F	**2**	**37**	**28**	**36**
Set G	**9**	**12**	**17**	**21**
Set H	**23**	**26**	**25**	**14**

Instruction Sheet

Task 1

Working with your partner, pick the 'Odd One Out'.

Write down the word, and the reason why is it the 'Odd One Out'.

Task 2

You should be able to see a pattern. The words have something in common.

Write down a Set from Task 1 and add another word from the Wordlist which has something in common – which keeps the 'Odd One Out' the same.

Task 3

On your own, try to put together your own Set of words with an 'Odd One Out'.

Swap your Set of words with your partner. See if you can work out each other's 'Odd One Out'.

Task 4

Now try to sort out all the words from the Word List into Sets with something in common.

Exemplar 2

Plains Indians

Context

This task was done with a mixed ability Y8 group. As I had only been teaching them for two months I had not really got them used to *teaching thinking*, and they were still wary of open tasks. The high achievers, apart from a couple of girls, were strangely subdued and most of the low achieving pupils were fairly well motivated, but there was good interaction between pupils of all abilities. They had enjoyed studying Plains Indians. A few of the boys were fairly obsessed with the gory bits, but I was surprised at how pro-Native American they were. It appeared that quite a few had seen the film *Dances with Wolves*. This activity was undertaken as the last task in the Unit to provide an interactive way of gaining an insight into their understanding: were they developing a real feel for this sad episode in American history? I had done several **Odd One Out** activities before, and I had an idea of the way that their own knowledge could suddenly surface and inform their reasoning.

> Pupils often have fixed images of 'the past' which are 'informed' by the media and are very hard to dispel.

Preparation

I produced the **Word List** by going through books and a textbook and adding a few words that I thought might help shake up their thoughts, such as 'Gold Rush', 'greed' and 'conservation'. I decided to make the first two Sets easy:

> A carefully 'stepped' planning sequence is required.

Crow – shield – bow and arrow – headdress;

Captain Benteen – Major Reno – General Custer – Red Cloud.

I then planned a much harder Set which was more ambiguous.

Launching

Unusually for me, I was mentally and physically well prepared. I took in a pack of playing cards. I held up 4♦, 5♦, 6♦ and 8♠ and asked which was the 'Odd One Out'. Fortunately I got the answer I expected – the 8 because it is a spade and black and others are diamonds and red. I then held up Jack♥, Jack♦, Jack♠ and Queen♠. They went for the obvious, the Queen, as the others were Jacks. I then held up 6♦, 7♥, 8♥, and 10♥. I introduced the third set by saying something like: *'OK, easy so far but what about this?'* This drew their attention to the fact that this was harder, and without much effort on my part I got two competing answers: 6♦ because it was not a heart; and 10♥ because it was not part of a run. I could then make the point that each card had three characteristics: a suit; a colour; and a denomination. And – depending on the game and the situation, the suit or the denomination could be more important. I could have made the point that an invisible characteristic, such as whether it was a trump or not, could be very important also, but I didn't. I then made a more general point that, for all sorts of reasons, being aware that most things had more than one characteristic was important. I used the example of a mobile phone. It is a means of communication, it is a fashion item, it is a health hazard (possibly) and it costs money to use. Each would be important in different contexts: an accident; looking cool; reducing health risk; and managing your budget.

> An example of using intriguing everyday props to 'draw' pupils into the task.

Instructions

We did the first one together. Some did not remember that the Crow were a tribe, but we got the general idea. I gave each group (mostly pairs) a GCSE textbook and told them on which pages to find the relevant chapter.

I then told them to work through the Sets. I emphasised that there might be more than one answer, that they should make sure that they could give a reason stating what characteristic the three had in common that the 'Odd One Out' lacked. I said that I would expect them to use the word 'characteristic' in giving their answers and reasons.

> Pupils were hereby encouraged to extend their vocabulary and to justify their reasoning.

I said that speed and finishing was not the point – it was the quality of their *thinking* that mattered.

Managing the activity

The start was painful. One group of three boys, one very bright and two about average, rushed through four Sets in about three minutes. Meanwhile about six pairs were plaguing me with 'Is this right?' and several others said that they didn't know various words. There was an air of discontent and resentment.

> Often pupils need 'warming up' and reminding that Thinking Skills activities do not equate to the 'correct-answer' syndrome.

So I stopped them and went over two points. Firstly, that there was not one correct answer, although there might be better answers – which was why they had to think about their reasons and not just go with the first thing that came into their heads. Secondly, if they were stuck on a word they should use their exercise books or the textbooks to check things out. I reminded them that the textbook had an index. In an encouraging tone I told them that they were intelligent and that they just needed to learn how to use their brains rather than mine because mine was rather old and worn out.

Things improved. By listening, I picked up that two groups had different answers for the third Set. One said that Indian Agent was the 'Odd One Out' because all the others were Indians and he was white. The other group said that Sitting Bull was the 'Odd One Out' because he was a real person whereas the others could be anyone. I relayed this difference to the whole class and they started to relax a bit as they accepted that there was more than one answer. Over the next twenty minutes as they discussed the Sets, some pairs seemed quite excited by the idea that there was no particular answer, which I found a bit bizarre. Had they been so conditioned by school to think only about correct answers? It got to the point where a few pairs were trying to generate obtuse answers.

One Set was: railroad – greed – buffalo – Gold Rush. One pair of boys had picked Gold Rush because it was two words and the others were only one word. I said that they should look for the best answer, but they did not want to budge, so I decided that I had to respect their reasoning, because that was what I was trying to encourage.

Those that finished the ten Sets were encouraged to make up their own Sets and exchange with other groups and this proved to be a very successful extension.

Debriefing

I had about 15 minutes left, which was never going to be enough. Nonetheless it was very useful to allow me to encourage and reinforce the value of reasoning and discussion. A few pupils seemed genuinely excited and liberated by the idea that there could be more than one answer and the general atmosphere was fairly animated in the discussion.

I asked groups in turn to give their 'Odd Ones Out', allowing others to come in if they had an alternative. I made them use the word 'characteristics' and I had to remind one pair that they had to explain what the three had in common that the fourth lacked. However we really changed gear when we got to 'railroad – greed – buffalo – Gold Rush'. I asked the boys who had picked Gold Rush and they gave their expected answer. As I anticipated, others quickly jumped in. Two girls said that it was buffalo because the others were to do with the White Man wanting the Indians' land. A mixed group of three then said that it was greed because the others were examples of greed, while greed was the general thing. The original pair protested that buffalo were not greedy and the reply was that shooting them for hides and leaving the bodies was, but this was countered with a claim that the word was 'buffalo' not 'shooting buffalo'. Just for 20 seconds they forgot that I was there – which I think was quite an achievement!

Rather hurriedly I set some homework that I hoped would consolidate the idea of characteristics. I told them to choose 4 words or terms from the list and space them out evenly on a page. For each they had to put six spokes radiating out. On each spoke they had to put a characteristic of that term, so that the six provided some kind of description or definition of the term. I used Sitting Bull as an example and suggested: Indian – Chief – warrior – bravery – coup – Little Big Horn. I made the point that these words were not just adjectives, some would be things that we associated with them. I needed more time to explain this to them, but the bell had gone. As it turned out some did this very well, a few put the first words that came into their heads and three did not do it at all claiming that they did not know what I meant. These 'Characteristic Wheels' provided a very good start to the next lesson.

Conscious reinforcement of the key objective and vocabulary building.

Consider the way in which homework helps reinforce the Thinking Skills Strategy.

Resource 4   **Word List**

1. warrior	18. bow and arrow
2. Cheyenne	19. Indian agent
3. cavalry	20. headdress
4. rifle	21. reservation
5. scalp	22. Major Reno
6. coups	23. Battle of Little Bighorn
7. Sitting Bull	24. buffalo
8. Crow	25. bravery
9. Holy Man	26. Sioux
10. horses	27. conservation
11. lodge	28. coup stick
12. Crazy Horse	29. General Custer
13. farming	30. Gold Rush
14. Captain Benteen	31. fort
15. railroad	32. pollution
16. greed	33. Wounded Knee
17. shield	34. ghost dance

Word List – Sets of Words

Set A	**8**	**17**	**18**	**20**
Set B	**12**	**14**	**22**	**29**
Set C	**1**	**7**	**9**	**19**
Set D	**10**	**13**	**25**	**28**
Set E	**13**	**27**	**30**	**32**
Set F	**15**	**16**	**24**	**30**
Set G	**19**	**21**	**31**	**34**
Set H	**3**	**4**	**9**	**31**

Resource 6   **Instruction sheet**

Task 1

What is the 'Odd One Out' in the following word Sets? There is not necessarily a correct answer, but you need to give a reason for why one is the 'Odd One Out'. What do the three have in common that the fourth does not have?

Task 2

Try to add one more word to each Set, if possible, which keeps the Odd One Out' the same.

Task 3

Make up a Set of your own and exchange them with another group. If their answer is different they are not wrong – they just have different reasons.

Trench Warfare

Context

This task was taught to a mixed ability Year 9 class. Although I had worked through several *Thinking Through History* Strategies before I sensed that many of the pupils were not that keen on the 'open-ended' nature of many of them. The idea of 'valid alternatives' seemed to worry the group – who seemed to operate more comfortably in the zone of the 'correct answer syndrome'. Nonetheless, I thought that the ideas behind an 'Odd One Out?' were worthy of perseverance.

Preparation

I created the **Word List** and related **Instruction Sheet** based upon key terms which we had studied within previous lessons – some of which were summarised upon a classroom 'word wall' display.

Launching

To ease the pupils into the Tasks, I decided to base the first Set of words around four familiar black and white photographs from *A Western Front Photo Pack* published by the Imperial War Museum, which we had used earlier:

Photo A   The muddy wastes of Paschendaele, 1917
Photo B   A British tank at Cambrai, 1917
Photo C   A German machine gun crew
Photo D   Indian troops undertaking rifle training

I explained that the idea of the exercise was to spot the 'Odd One Out'.

> This is a technique to tap into the pupils' visual memories of past learning.

First, look for the characteristic features of the things shown in the photos. Next, having established these characteristics, apply the same test to each photo/word in turn, and thereby identify the 'Odd One Out'. Certainly the visual images 'kick started' the pupils into talking: *'Well, they are all about the War'* ... *'Three photos show things made to kill people'*. I next posed a recall question *'But earlier, didn't we find out that mud could kill soldiers as well?'* Some thought about that before replying *'Yes, but mud is different – it's not made to kill people, it's natural'*. *'That's right, it's not made by some people to kill other people'*.

> This is an example of 'talk' being used to develop pupils' understanding through 'stepping up' the question demands and task difficulty.

I sensed by now that the class had the idea, and was ready for the task.

We did just one more together without the aid of any photos: mustard gas – bully beef – heavy artillery – mining.

Some pupils had forgotten what bully beef was, others were mystified about what mining had to do with trench warfare. Clearly, extra support was going to be needed. I gave each pair of pupils a Key Stage 3 topic book and reminded them to use both the contents, glossary and index pages to speed up any necessary searches for information.

I then told them to work through the Sets. I emphasised that there might be more than one answer, that they should make sure that they could give a reason stating what characteristic the three had in common that the fourth one lacked. I said that I would expect them to use the word 'characteristic' in giving their answers and reasons. I said that speed and finishing was not the point – it was the quality of their thinking.

Managing the activity

Initially, most pairs set to work with gusto. The early 'Odd Ones Out', which mostly focused upon the characteristics of weapons or trench construction, caused little confusion. Set D, however, took the context away from the 'mud, blood and guts' and forced pupils' thinking towards another theme within a different context. Immediately, judging from the forest of hands up, I could see that a whole class intervention would be necessary. *'Look, for those of you who are a bit stuck on the Set D words – just think back to the work we did on why Wilf Smith joined up'*. (A **Mystery** along very similar lines may be found in *Chapter 5* page 64). The idea of past-referencing to previous work involving an individual seemed to assist their thought processes.

> Once again, pupils' new understanding is moved forward by, firstly, revisiting previous work about a similar context.

The pairs worked well as I continued to quietly circulate, 'listening in' to interesting points and making 'mental notes' of which pairs I might be able to 'springboard' profitable lines of enquiry, or counter-arguments from through teacher questioning later in the session.

The pairs who finished their ten Sets were encouraged to make up some more, based upon the same idea. These were then exchanged with another pair, thereby providing a very useful extension for the 'fast finishers'.

Debriefing

Although I had only 10 minutes left, which was far too short a time span, I did manage to use the pupils' responses to reinforce the value of thinking and reasoning through talking. I asked each pair to offer their 'Odd Ones Out', reminding them to use the term 'characteristic' in their explanation as to why three words were similar whilst the fourth word was – in their view – different.

This is an interesting example of the flexibility of the **Odd One Out** Strategy.

Discussion became quite heated once we turned to Set F: barbed wire – propaganda – No Man's Land – 'Over the Top'. At this point the terms provided an interesting example of divergent thinking. When asked directly for their 'Odd One Out' several pairs plumped for 'propaganda'. When asked for their reasons, opinions varied, but the essential characteristics linking the other three terms were expressed thus: *'they are all to do with… actual fighting'*, *'or bits of the trench system'*. One pair totally disagreed: *'We think the 'Odd One Out' is barbed wire … because it's a man-made item (used for defending ground) …the other three terms are linked because they are all 'ideas'(to do with attacking and capturing ground)*. Since this was precisely an example of the differing reasoning I hoped might emerge, I was more than pleased to allow the discussion to tease out related issues. At one point there was a period of genuine pair to pair, pupil to pupil discussion without reference to my presence in the room!

These are all interesting counter-explanations based – as they were – upon appropriate evidence.

To conclude the lesson I asked the class to think about:

- what skills had they used within the lesson to complete the task?
- where else, within other topics or lessons at school, could the idea of looking for similarities of characteristics be useful?

Word List

1. mud	19. Belgium
2. mustard gas	20. heavy artillery
3. tanks	21. gas mask
4. trench	22. shell shock
5. volunteer	23. recruit
6. bombardment	24. Battle of the Somme
7. propaganda	25. lice
8. bully beef	26. rats
9. enlist	27. absent without leave
10. trench foot	28. rifle
11. Blighty	29. mining
12. Britain	30. sandbags
13. barbed wire	31. General Haig
14. duckboard	32. France
15. wound	33. 'Over the Top'
16. 'No Man's Land'	34. recover
17. Germany	35. poetry
18. machine gun	36. disease

Resource 8   **Word List – Sets of Words**

Set A	1	3	18	28
Set B	2	8	20	29
Set C	4	14	19	30
Set D	9	23	5	31
Set E	17	6	12	32
Set F	13	7	16	33
Set G	11	21	15	34
Set H	24	10	22	35
Set I	25	27	26	36

Concept Maps

3 Concept Maps

Rationale

Concept mapping has a considerable history and research pedigree as a tool for improving understanding. The history lies largely in science; a large number of research studies attest to its varied benefits. The Strategy has five particular advantages:

1. It is highly visual and encourages pupils to make connections between concepts and thus produce their own key ideas in a 'big picture'.
2. It stimulates pupils to use what they already know and can give some sense of ownership in learning.
3. It can be the basis for planning writing, as the map allows pupils to trace causal chains between concepts – it can be a great tool for KS3 literacy.
4. It is highly differentiated, as some pupils may work only with 4 concepts on cards while others work with more.
5. The visual nature of the tasks means that some pupils retain the image of the map in their long-term memory, which acts as a very powerful gateway to recall and understanding.

One of the drawbacks of vigorous testing regimes, which are in the ascendancy, is that they atomise knowledge into easily assessed units. We tend to assess that which is easy to test. **Concept Maps** are a wonderful diagnostic assessment tool as they give insights into the quality of pupils' understanding and the number of links that pupils are able to forge.

Finally, it should be mentioned that because concepts provide a 'big picture' they are therefore an invaluable planning tool for teachers. Your planning **Concept Map** should contain the central concepts in the topic onto which you can plot the main ideas or principles.

The principles outlined above fit very well with much recent work upon establishing brief – yet rigorous – overviews of topics by developing pupils' appreciation of the 'big picture', or 'key idea' (see Counsell, 2000 and Riley, 2000).

Equally, **Concept Maps** can act as a powerful tool to select, and organise 'topic relevant' concepts (see Arthur, 2000 and Counsell, 2000) as well as creating one possible structure for pupils to produce sustained, extended writing in an analytical and discursive genre.

Asking pupils to transform their existing knowledge and understanding into a diagrammatical format develops a worthwhile skill.

The benefits of this Strategy lie in revealing where pupils' confusions and misunderstandings are most deeply embedded.

Making links and connections are central to success in history in the context of NC, GCSE, AS and A2 demands.

The Strategy is flexible: it can be deployed at the beginning, middle or end of a Unit. It is also an excellent revision technique.

Diagnostic assessment concerns, linked to pupil target setting can readily emerge from this Strategy.

The Abolition of Slavery

Context

This **Concept Map** was used as part of the KS3 scheme of work: 'Britain 1750 -1900'. It was attempted in the Spring Term of Year 9. For several lessons this mixed-ability Year 9 class had been learning about the development of the British Empire and its involvement in the slave trade. Year 9 had proven to be very enthusiastic about this subject and would always ask further questions and would listen intently to the story of the African slaves on their journey through the middle passage.

I decided to use this activity because I wanted to pull together all of the knowledge which these pupils had and to develop their understanding of why slavery ended.

The following learning outcomes were targeted when planning this activity:

- knowledge and understanding of *who* tried to end the slave trade;
- understanding of *why* these people wanted to end the slave trade;
- understanding of *how* these people and events are not solitary causes, and that they are interlinked;
- the ability to explain reasons *orally* and in the more traditional written form;
- to develop the pupils' *vocabulary* and thereby enhance their *literacy* skills, particularly for the less able.

Preparation

1 Since the class were going to work in groups of four, the dynamics required prior thought. I decided upon a mix of friendship and abilities within each sub-group.
2 Decide upon the *key question*. I decided to pose: '*Why was the slave trade abolished?*
3 Give each group an A3 piece of sugar paper.

This activity takes very little physical preparation.

> The key question needs careful thought. It needs to be intriguing and challenging yet, at the same time, one which encompasses prior work and is deliverable.

Launching

This class was already familiar with the individuals and groups who contributed to the abolition of the slave trade. They knew how it had ended and a little as to why it had ended. I wanted them to be more aware of the motivating factors behind the actions of individuals. As a class we discussed what a **cause** was and what an **effect** was. We then continued to discuss the reasons why people act in a particular way, and what were the motivating factors that influenced individuals to follow a certain path. We used simple modern analogies – within pupils' experience – such as the *causes* why students forgot their homework. I informed the class that we were going to decide, in groups, why the slave trade was abolished. Also, that some of the causes will be connected and may have influenced other causes.

> The use of modern analogies, within the pupils' own experiences, is a valuable **bridging** device (see page 138).

Instructions

1 The class was organised into groups and each group was provided with a sheet of sugar paper and some coloured pens.
2 The class was instructed that it was essential that they worked as a group and that they considered each other's ideas.
3 Each group was told that they must be prepared to present their **Concept Map** to the rest of the class and to explain their findings.
4 I put an example of a **Concept Map** on the board and asked the class to offer any causes they could think of for why the slave trade was abolished. These causes were written on the board around the key question. I asked the class if they could think of any connections between the causes which they had suggested. One pupil offered the link between the French Revolution and Toussaint L'Ouverture. The connection was that Toussaint L'Ouverture was inspired by the ideas of the French revolution: of equality and liberty. These ideas inspired the black slaves on the island of St Domingue to revolt against their plantation owners. I added the connection and the pupils' words to the board.

> **Modelling**, to establish key causes and links between causes, is time well spent.

The pupils were then instructed to copy the basic format (see *Resource 1*) onto their sugar paper and then, as a group, to discuss any connections between the causes. Next, they were instructed to draw a line between these connections and then to write an explanation connection along each of these connection lines.

Managing the activity

As I circulated around the class I realised that many pupils knew which causes were connected but were finding difficulty in explaining the connection. At this point I would try to tease out of the group why they had drawn a connection between two particular causes. If this did not work, then I would try to place them on the correct path without, if possible, providing them with the explanation.

Debriefing

As a result of my earlier monitoring and interventions I was aware of which groups had reached a higher level of understanding and had fully explained their connections on the **Concept Map**. I asked one group if they would present their **Concept Map** to the rest of the class. Fortunately this posed no major problem as this class have a healthy and supportive relationship with each other. (If this had not been the case I would have asked each group to explain their findings to the group that was placed near them). As the exemplar group presented their **Concept Map**, I made sure that they were explaining to the rest of the class why they had made that connection.

I concluded by asking the class what they had learnt in the lesson. The responses ranged from being able to express their beliefs, working in groups, to understanding that there is usually more than one cause for an event taking place, and that these causes are usually connected in different ways.

Follow-up

The pupils transferred their findings into an extended piece of writing upon: *'Why was the slave trade abolished?'* The work that was produced was mixed. Some higher ability pupils produced excellent work which showed how they had used the **Concept Map** to structure their thoughts prior to writing. The less able managed to produce reasonable accounts and were beginning to link a few causes, in a non-narrative manner – more than is normally the case. I do feel, however, that had they been provided with a summary style 'proforma' of their **Concept Map** (see *Resource 1*) this would have aided the less able, who were relying upon their short-term memory of the lesson.

Adapting the Strategy

This particular topic lends itself to an exploration of the fundamental concept of human rights and its related sub-concepts through the emotionally 'safer' distance of time, place, people and events. The study of slavery offers a splendid springboard to compare different ideas, beliefs and attitudes prevalent at the time of 'the slave trade', as well as to plot how they altered through time and circumstance. QCA's *Scheme of Work Unit 15* on *Black Peoples of America*, designed specifically to support Year 9, offers a great number of worthwhile ideas.

As well as the 'history' aspects, such a topic provides an excellent vehicle to link NC history-based work to the impending citizenship requirements at Key Stage 3, notably:

Knowledge and Understanding

1 Pupils should be taught about:
   a) human rights.

Develop Skills of Enquiry and Communication

2 Pupils should be taught to:
   a) think about political, moral, social and cultural issues, problems and events;
   b) justify orally or in writing a personal opinion;
   c) contribute to group and class discussion, and take part in debates.

Develop Skills in Participation

3 Pupils should be taught to:
   a) use their imaginations to consider other peoples' experiences and be able to think about, express, and explain views that are not their own.

This is just one example of how appropriate *thinking* Strategies and history Strategies may simultaneously offer pupils a 'triple whammy' of worthwhile experiences through history, citizenship and Key Skills.

Why was the slave trade abolished? Key factors.

Declining profits on plantations

Working class petitions

Toussaint L'Ouverture

Slave rebellions

Why was the slave trade abolished?

Grey's Whig Government

Accounts of conditions on slave ships and plantations

Wilberforce

Climate of reform

French Revolution

Why did the Japanese bomb Pearl Harbour?

Context

This activity was set up for a top band GCSE group. They were studying the AQA *Modern World History* course, *Syllabus B*. The group consists of 21 pupils who are aiming for final grades A*- C. It consists of 3 pupils who have been identified as 'more able' by the school policy. The group itself is quite lively and high-spirited and has gelled well. They are all well motivated and fun to teach. This was the first **Concept Map** that I had used with this particular class, although some had used other *thinking* activities before. The background information and the idea for this task came from *Peace and War* (*SHP History Series*, John Murray).

The intended learning outcomes of this whole class activity were:

- to understand the reasons why the Japanese bombed Pearl Harbour;
- to appreciate that causation is complex, and that to explain an event involves understanding how and why causes are linked – rather than seeing factors in isolation;
- to improve the pupils' level of thinking;
- to encourage different members of the group to contribute orally to the ensuing discussion;
- to 'cash in' pupils' understanding through setting a follow-up written task. (I felt that in the light of recent 'past paper' homework many pupils were not making important links and connections in their written answers and thus not achieving the higher levels in the mark schemes).

I also feel it is important to get over the 'them and us' feeling that many of the pupils have: that the Germans or Japanese are the 'bad guys' and the British and Americans are the 'good guys'. Hence, I wanted to highlight and emphasise that Japan had its own grievances with America which were just as valid as America's grievances with Japan.

Lastly, I hoped that once the pupils had completed the **Concept Map** they would be able to internalise the *process* and repeat it at home when doing individual work on other related topics.

Preparation

The preparation for this task was straightforward and was not time-consuming. I took the background information and the key factors from the *Peace and War* textbook (pp180-181). Before the lesson I had prepared my own version of the **Concept Map** as a guideline for myself and to familiarise myself with the task so that I could focus the pupils more specifically.

Launching

I put summarised factors around the edge of the board and left space for any others that the pupils could come up with themselves. I put the *key question 'Why did the Japanese bomb Pearl Harbour?'* at the centre. I then brainstormed the pupils to see what perceptions they had as to why Japan became involved in World War Two (see *Resource 2*). They came up with suggestions: the failure of the League of Nations; Japan was already at war with China. I added these to the board. Other suggestions were made, but after discussion the pupils decided they weren't directly linked with the question.

We read and discussed the information and looked at the map in the book. We also looked at a globe and, through doing so, visualised just how close Japan was to America. This was an excellent ploy in showing the pupils the proximity of the two countries and helped them to realise and understand that America and Japan had their own grievances. Through questioning, it became clear that before this activity most pupils assumed that America came into the war simply to help Britain in the war against Hitler and Germany.

Instructions

1 I told the pupils the key question and focused their attention on the board.
2 I then reinforced what we had discussed in the light of reading the background information from the textbook and asked them to give me a reason why Japan had joined the war. They decided that there was not just one reason but many.

Nevertheless, as with all Thinking Skills activities, a suitable knowledge-base is required by the pupils.

A very worthwhile stage, to force pupils – 'literally' – to see the situation differently other than from their usual anglocentric perspective.

Such pupil misconceptions are notoriously hard to shift.

Again, teacher modelling to reveal the objective and method through talk is helpful.

Research studies indicate that pupils appreciate opportunities to re-interpret their existing understanding in diagrammatic forms.

Thinking Through History

This led me to the aim of the lesson: to demonstrate that events have many causes and that those causes do not happen in isolation, but are linked together.

3 I explained that they were going to do a **Concept Map** as a class so that they could share their ideas. The point of the **Concept Map** was to show them how causation was linked.

To illustrate how a **Concept Map** worked, I led them through the first link: I randomly selected one of the points from the board, which happened to be *'Japan wanted to build a strong empire'*. I asked them: *'How would this affect their foreign policy and their attitude to other countries?'* The pupils said: *'They would be aggressive and would be looking for opportunities to invade/attack other countries'*. I then asked them to link this idea to another card on the board, which they did with ease. I wrote this on the board and asked them to fill in their own copies as the lesson progressed. Once they had done the first one they understood how it worked and there was no stopping them. They came up with many different links and were able to explain why they thought they were linked together. This in turn allowed them to argue and debate with each other and thus stretched their thinking and explaining techniques, since it was made clear that they had to be able to justify what they were saying.

Managing the activity

The management of this activity was easy. Part of this, however, was due to the co-operative nature and size of the group. As far as my own role was concerned, whilst the pupils drew up their **Concept Maps** I found it especially useful to circulate – but at arm's length. Instead of jumping in to support, it proved helpful to simply eavesdrop upon discussions. Just occasionally, when I thought it might push pupils' thoughts forward, I asked groups to explain specific links.

Debriefing

When the **Concept Map** was finished I asked the pupils what they thought they had learnt. The general feedback was that they understood *what* the factors were and also *why* they were linked. The visual format made the links between causation much more obvious and easier to understand. This helped them to feel more confident when arguing their point with other members of the group.

They also said that they would be able to use the strategy of a **Concept Map** at home when doing past papers and in general revision of topics. I enjoyed the lesson immensely and was surprised and delighted when the quietest pupil in the class, whom I have difficulty in getting to contribute orally, 'came to life'. He was confident, animated and had his hand up for the whole lesson. The pupils' subsequent written answers were generally concise – but also linked key factors and provided a balanced answer in a more focused question-specific manner.

A practical example of **bridging**, or **transfer**.

They were able to include more than one point of view as to why the Japanese bombed Pearl Harbour, thus showing a higher level of thinking and writing. I could not claim a uniform improvement but I felt that most of the group had made improvements.

A sequence of positive outcomes.

Follow-up

For homework, I asked the pupils to write a brief account answering the *key question*: *'Why did the Japanese bomb Pearl Harbour?'* Since then I have also asked them to use the technique of a **Concept Map** to help them structure their own homework. For a less able group I would offer a proforma listing the key arguments, to be filled in during the activity. I would explain and approach the activity in the same way, for the benefit of the brainstorm followed by pupils creating their own **Concept Map** on the board. This is not a difficult task to do. The pupils can see the way a **Concept Map** is constructed. This then aids the transfer of skills, enabling them to easily do this themselves at home.

Resource 2 Why did the Japanese bomb Pearl Harbour? Key factors.

Japan wanted to build a strong empire in Asia

Japan had appointed a warlike General as Prime Minister

Japan believed the Americans would not fight back

Japan believed a war with America was inevitable and wanted to strike first

Why did the Japanese bomb Pearl Harbour?

Japan was already at war with China

America provoked Japan into war by imposing sanctions and making impossible demands

Japan needed raw materials like oil. It could only get them by invading oil fields in South East Asia

The failure of the League of Nations had not stopped Japan before

Lifelines

4 Lifelines

Rationale

History makes considerable use of line graphs as a means to represent data. Graphs are familiar territory for history teachers. Pupils are customarily asked simple data response questions, or to describe the graph, or maybe they are just asked to draw a graph from a set of data. These tasks have their place. However, use of graphs rarely excites or creates debate and argument. Graphs are not unpacked as a particular form of representing reality. Often they are simply used as a means to organise, represent and communicate matters of 'hard' data concerning quantity, for example, the increase of industrial production against time, or the rate of rural/urban population change through time. **Lifelines** can change pupils' way of looking at graphs.

The three Exemplars using Thinking Skills graphs within this Chapter demonstrate **Lifelines**. They offer pupils access into very different ways of studying historical topics. They are relatively simple activities to plan and manage, but the outcomes can be profound.

They use 'emotions' as the unit of analysis. This should, however, be regarded as a virtue not a vice. **Lifelines** are based around past peoples' motives, intentions, reactions, attitudes, values and beliefs. Within history these 'softer' sources offer fertile gateways into discussion and interpretations. And, importantly, they use a diagrammatic format: all that is required is the plotting of a point on a graph, rather than writing.

In **Lifelines** pupils are presented with episodes in a short or long term narrative. They are asked to plot these episodes as a point on a scale of positive to negative emotion. These points can then be joined up to provide a trace of emotion over time. The beauty of the Strategy is that the response of a variety of protagonists can be displayed. In **Lifelines** pupils are asked to plot the feelings or emotions of an individual over a number of episodes. It is a particular form of time line. **Lifelines** also encourage the interpretation of events through the eyes of individuals or groups. All pupils are aware of their own emotions and how emotions fluctuate in response to events; this understanding can be used to encourage them to think through how other people felt as events unfolded. They are encouraged to see time periods, short or long, as differentiated in terms of how they were experienced.

In **Lifelines** pupils draw a line graph – or are given a pre-printed one. They are given *statements* relating to a given theme, sequence of events or what people might have said. They have to decide where on the graph (at what time point) it was most likely to have occurred.

One advantage of **Lifelines** is that they give the figures and the axes of the graph some real context, and allow students to make connections between the abstraction of the graph on the page and the people and events that lie behind it. Whilst ordinary line graphs show the relationships between just two variables, such as time and number of migrants, **Lifelines** can give a reminder that other variables, such as education, politics and public health are interacting with the ones depicted in the graph. **Lifelines** therefore greatly assist pupils in constructing meaning from the graph. They make students think and talk – and disagree with each other and you. They encourage them to ask more questions, and even on occasions to stay behind after the bell. They make students look at graphs in a totally new light. They are extremely flexible. Exactly the same resources can be used for a Y7 and a Y13 class – which says much about their potential for differentiation by outcome.

Thinking Skills are employed:

Reasoning skills, which enable pupils to give reasons for their opinions and decisions and to use precise language to explain what they think.

Creative thinking skills, which enable pupils to generate ideas and apply imagination in the search for an alternative solution.

Evaluation skills, which enable pupils to evaluate information and develop informed criteria for judging their own and others' thinking and ideas.

> This process can readily tap into the pupils' 'emotional intelligence'.

> The issue of how much background context the pupils need in relation to **Lifelines** is an issue to consider.

> **Lifelines** can be excellent starting points for rival interpretations of individuals, or groups.

The Peasants' Revolt

Context

This **Lifeline** was used with a mixed ability Year 7 group within their 'Britain 1066-1500' studies at the end of a Unit of work on the Black Death and the Peasants' Revolt. Because of timetabling problems this was a split class whom I saw for 50 minutes for the last lesson on a Friday (rarely the best time of the week!). Nevertheless, they were a well-motivated and lively group. Earlier they had studied the Black Death and its results, which they had then classified into short and long-term effects. Previously, they had also looked at the causes of the Peasants' Revolt and watched a video on its events. The activity assumes that pupils understand the term 'villein' and know about the 'Statute of Labourers'.

> It is useful for pupils to have a relevant knowledge base; so that the Strategy can be targeted to deepen their understanding through a process of internalisation.

I decided to use a **Lifeline** for this particular piece of work for several reasons. Firstly, I wanted pupils to understand the causes of the Peasants' Revolt. I hoped to give pupils an insight into the plight of the peasants and consider the pressures they faced. Secondly, I wanted them to have knowledge of the events in London in 1381, and to understand how the peasants might have felt when they realised they had been tricked. Thirdly, I hoped that in using the same basic *statements* to create their **Lifelines**, the pupils might learn something of how events could be interpreted differently according to the point of view of both the peasants and the King. Developing empathy across the different viewpoints is useful. This activity can be used either to teach the events and the causes of the revolt during the Unit (as in this example) or used later as a revision or assessment exercise.

> This Strategy reinforces 'cause': a 'big concept' in history.

> This 'human' dilemma may give rise to **cognitive conflict** – a powerful learning device.

Preparation

The preparation of the episodes needs some careful thought – in terms of their number, their language level and their capacity to be interpreted in different ways.

Launching

The activity was introduced by explaining that the lesson would involve the pupils working in pairs. Pupils should understand that the work they would be doing would not produce a 'correct' answer as such, but instead would involve them 'tapping into' the emotions of people involved in an event in the past, and trying to represent those peoples' feelings by plotting points upon a line graph. I emphasised the importance of discussion and said they had to try and reach agreement in their pairs.

> These ideas of 'alternative answers' and 'conflict resolution' are embedded in many Strategies.

I demonstrated on the board how they should construct the **Lifeline**. The horizontal axis is designed to plot 'time' and 'events'. Care needs to be taken in explaining that the frequency of events upon this axis may well not be uniform, and that the scale may be a variable one. The vertical axis represents 'feelings', ranging along a continuum from +5 to 0, and then down to –5. These represent emotions: +5 being 'ecstasy', and –5 being the 'depths of despair'.

To tap in to the pupils' emotional feelings of what such terms might mean, I drew upon an analogy. Pupils were encouraged to recall the range of their own feelings when their local team, Newcastle United, won their FA Cup semi-final in 1999, only to lose in their second successive FA Cup Final to the treble-winning Manchester United.

> A powerful (if painful) example of **bridging**.

Instructions

1 Explain the aim. I expressed this as a key question: *'How would the peasants be feeling at each stage of the Peasants Revolt?'*

2 Ask pupils to draw a vertical line the length of 10 lines in their exercise book, and a horizontal line 12 cm in length, giving 1cm per event. (A word of warning: have plenty of rulers on hand!) The date of each event can then be marked along the horizontal axis.

3 The pairs should discuss, then plot with a cross, the peasants' reaction to each statement in turn on the **Lifeline**.

4 By way of example, I read the first statement, and asked the pupils for possible peasant responses. Then, through questioning, I teased out where they might mark this response upon their graph.

> A useful ploy, whenever possible.

(Note: at this stage it would be useful to obtain more than one opinion to demonstrate to the pupils that there is not simply one correct answer, eg 'relief at surviving the plague', 'looking forward to higher wages for working on the land' and so on...)

5   Ask students to work in pairs and complete their graphs. Various possibilities exist from 'cutting and sticking' the statements to simply placing small crosses at the appropriate point on the graph. Another variation is to show individual peasants' emotional reactions to events with a sequence of smiley or sad faces (stickers?). Remind them that they must be able to justify and explain the reasons for their choice afterwards.

Managing the activity

I found it useful to start this activity by recapping, and so did not have the full 50 minutes. Pupils began their activity, and I circulated the room helping and encouraging where necessary. A useful ploy was to encourage them to relate the exercise to events in their own lives. Encourage pupils to read the whole sheet through before they begin plotting, so that they don't automatically give the first bad event a score of –5. Some of my pupils planned it out in rough first – which is fine – although the task consequently took longer. As extension work, the pupils who finished early were asked to plot a comparable **Lifeline** for King Richard, starting the graph with the third event, his accession to the throne.

Debriefing

The feedback was, for me, the most worthwhile part of the lesson. Initially, I decided to go through this on an event-by-event basis. I was amazed at the variety of responses and the quality of the answers. Pupils had thought of things which hadn't occurred to me and they were all able to contribute to the discussion. This selection of pupil comments attests to their enjoyment:

> 'It was helpful because we knew how they felt'.
>
> 'I enjoyed the lesson because ... you could talk about things with your partner and say what you thought'.
>
> 'It helped me understand the peasants' life more. I really enjoyed working in pairs and sharing ideas'.

Unfortunately, I began to run out of time so discussed just the high points and the low points from their graphs. This too worked well as there were many differences of opinion.

As a follow-up, or if time permits in your lesson, you could take the discussion further. Pupils could be asked 'How did they arrive at their decisions?' 'Were their decisions based upon care for themselves?' 'Did they think of themselves and their families, or were other considerations important?' 'Did they take the 'bigger picture' into account?' 'Did they think in the short term of the long term, for instance were they glad when the tax collectors were killed or were they worried about possible reprisals from the King?'

Analysis of the pupils' decision-making process is important. They should be encouraged to consider how they made their decisions.

Follow-up

As a homework task, pupils were asked to justify their decisions, by translating their understanding of the Peasants' Revolt – achieved through the **Lifeline** – into a written account. You could differentiate by asking more able pupils to include their decisions for all the dates, whilst the less able could be asked to justify decisions according to the high and low points on their graphs. For pupils who require support, you could provide a scaffolded sheet in the form of a persuasive writing frame to help get them started.

---

*A mixture of **metacognitive** comments and opinions.*

It can be productive to widen out the pupil responses towards the 'big picture' and the individual situation.

*A suitable case for **differentiation** by group work.*

The Peasants' Revolt: Statements

1348	The Black Death kills one third of the population.
1351	The Government introduces the Statute of Labourers.
1377	King Richard II comes to power aged 10. He introduces a poll tax to pay for the war with France.
1378	John Ball, a priest, begins to talk of differences between rich and poor. He is put in prison.
1381, March	After raising the tax twice, the King orders that anyone refusing to pay the tax should be put in prison.
1381, May	Villagers in Essex kill some tax collectors.
1381, 6 June	Rebel peasants in Kent, led by Wat Tyler, seize Rochester Castle.
1381, 7 June	They free John Ball.
1381, 12 June	The peasants arrive in London and demand the King gets rid of his advisers. The peasants run wild in London, smashing and burning the advisers' houses.
1381, 14 June	Richard meets the rebels at Mile End. He tells them to go home and promises they will be free.
1381, 15 June	Some peasants have stayed in London. They have killed the advisers and demand to meet the King. They meet him at Smithfield. The peasants' leader Wat Tyler is killed. King Richard promises they could be free if they go home.
1381, late summer	The leaders of the peasants are captured and hung! Richard says 'Villeins ye are, and villeins ye shall remain'.

Exemplar 2

Germ

Context

I created this **Lifeline** to illustrate one particular theme within our GCSE Schools' History Project course 'Medicine through Time'. It is designed to cover the whole 'development through time' aspect from prehistoric times to the present day. I taught it to a GCSE mixed ability Year 10 class who suffered from unbelievable apathy. This came at the end of the medicine Unit, in the Spring of Year 10. By this time the pupils were fed up with medicine and not motivated about revising for their forthcoming school exams. It was used as a revision exercise before their Year 10 exam.

My main aims behind this **Lifeline** were:

- to get my pupils to think!
- to engage with the material and discuss it;
- to work upon an exercise with a definite start and finish, to give the pupils a definite structure within which to develop their understanding of the topic;
- to remind them of some important developments in medicine;
- to improve pupils' motivation by presenting information in a 'different' manner.

Preparation

Care was taken in order not to give too much away in the *statements*. The statements need to be quite open ended so that pupils *do* have to think. The statements work best if they generate discussion and disagreement, although it is not always possible to do this.

Launching

I introduced the activity by explaining to the pupils that this was a revision exercise and that they would be working in pairs. (It may be useful to pair a less able pupil with a more able one to help their confidence, although clearly it is important that both pupils contribute to the discussion). I emphasised the importance of pupil talk and that in their pairs they should aim for agreement, although maybe – at times – arrived at through argument. The pupils were familiar with **Lifelines** and recalled their essential purpose. Nevertheless, as I expected, the students began to laugh when asked to imagine that they were a germ and that the point of the exercise was to plot their (the germ's) emotional reactions to medical changes through time!

Instructions

For step-by-step instructions refer to Exemplar 1 on page 39.

1 Draw a graph on the board (or use an OHP acetate) and ask the students to replicate it into their books.
2 Make sure they are sitting in pairs. I decided to group by friendship pairings.
3 Give out the worksheets. Allow the pupils 5 minutes to read. Ask them not to write anything yet, but simply to read the statements through to each other.
4 Next, by way of example, ask a pupil for her/his first response and plot it on the graph on the board.
5 Ask pupils to work through their statements, taking care to work out why they are awarding the emotion they are, and how this makes sense in relation to the others, so they can contribute to the debriefing.

For extra support pupils could, if necessary, refer to their prior work, text/topic books, CD-Roms and a range of 'Medicine Through Time' websites.

Managing the activity

As I circulated around the room, I asked a few pupils who looked a little lost what they thought the main aim of a germ would be. They suggested several impressive motives including '*to kill people*', '*to breed*', '*to be undiscovered*'. This helped them to understand what to do and get started. It may be useful to stop the class and discuss this to help prompt some of the less able. You may prefer to do this at the start, or even during the debrief. I had a 50 minute lesson and found this ample time for the whole process. As pupils started to complete their **Lifeline**, I asked them to justify their decisions in their books. Some planned this in rough first, writing it into books when they had reached agreement with their partner.

Lifelines such as this can be a stimulating Strategy to 'look afresh' at well-worn topics.

This holds good for all Thinking Skills Strategies.

This focus upon thinking derived from paired talk is a central objective.

This idea is full of intrigue and, therefore, more motivating.

An important point: offer pupils advance organisers such as these.

Debriefing

This is often the most worthwhile part of the activity. With this particular **Lifeline** there were few main areas of disagreement about content, and the pupils had picked out the points I had hoped they would identify. However, it was really useful for their revision to hear the reasons and thoughts of the other pupils. I was also pleased because all the students were able to participate and give their opinions in more depth and with more elaborated responses than usual. One thing which did come across was that the pupils found it fun and a bit of a laugh! I myself had been a little unsure of doing it like this – was it too silly? I asked a colleague: he thought it would be useful. Hence, I was fascinated to read these pupils' comments:

> 'It was good in that the questions made you think back to previous work, eg the question you asked me about cholera'.
>
> 'I really enjoyed it. It made you think more about it than if you were just writing an essay'.
>
> 'Trying to think like a germ is cool'.
>
> 'I think the game was good. I learnt a lot. If you think you're a germ and feel like a germ you have a better understanding of what to do. Cool game!'
>
> 'I liked being a germ. It was better than a normal lesson'.
>
> 'I like it and thought it was a good way of learning'.
>
> 'It was quite easy … it was good, and fun'.

Even one of the less enthusiastic wrote 'It was OK' (praise indeed!).

> The length of pupils' responses are a measure of the success of the Strategy.

> The application of previous knowledge is evident.

> It is possible that the Strategy motivated many since it accessed an alternative learning style – the iconic, or visual.

Follow-up

This can be writing in their reasons, or selecting some of the statements for some in-depth revision. Planning for follow-up was limited in this instance with it being a self-contained revision lesson.

Adapting the Strategy

I have since developed more **Lifelines** for use with this group. They have covered the long-term causes of the Irish Conflict, with students plotting the emotions of Catholics, Protestants and the British Government on the same graph. They have also studied settlers in the American West and their conflict with the Plains Indians.

Resource 2   The Causes and Cures of Disease: Overview

This piece of work is designed to be an enjoyable summary of one aspect of the 'Medicine Through Time' course.

Imagine that you are a germ! Think carefully about your chances, opportunities (and perhaps feelings!) at the following times in the following places.

Mark your responses on a graph, using the scale –5 for deepest darkest depression, up to +5 for your happiest, most wonderful moments.

Explain your answers carefully, point by point, underneath your graph.

If you are unsure about some of these things then you may use your textbook to help. Work in pairs for this. Your discussion and decisions are the most important parts.

1	Prehistoric England

2	The Roman Empire

3	Medieval York

4	1665, London

5	1799, Edward Jenner develops vaccination

6	1831, Sunderland in the year that cholera arrived

7	1861, the germ theory is published by Louis Pasteur

8	Robert Koch identifies specific bacteria causing specific diseases

9	The 1890s, Lister uses carbolic acid in surgery to prevent infection

10	1914-1918, the trenches of the Western Front

11	1928, penicillin is discovered

12	The 1930s, sulphonamide drugs (magic bullets) are developed

13	1942, penicillin is mass-produced

14	1980/1990s, some germs become resistant to some antibiotics

The Rise of Hitler

Context

The activity was set as a revision exercise for the GCSE history syllabus covering Units 2 to 4 of the second paper, including the topics 'Hitler and the growth of the Nazi party up to 1933' to 'Nazi rule in Germany'. This activity is also suitable for Key Stage 3 history within the context of 'A World Study After 1900'.

The activity was trialled with a Y11 mixed ability set of 25 pupils. The pupils' ability ranged from potential A grade to non exam entry. Due to the class dynamics, I do often have problems in developing class discussion work, because there is a distinct reluctance to share knowledge or opinions. While studying these Units previously there were many general misunderstandings, or biased views amongst the pupils, with regard to Hitler and Hitler's actions. Loose comments, revealing underlying xenophobic stereotypes and attitudes, were often shouted out in class as soon as Hitler's name was mentioned.

> Such Thinking Skills Strategies are often a useful vehicle to explore pupils' misconceptions and stereotypes.

My aims, therefore, for introducing the **Lifeline** were to use it as a form of revision for the work being covered in the study Units. I hoped that pupils would gain an insight into the experience of the vast majority of the German population who had little option but to submit to the excesses of Nazi rule.

Planning

The **Lifeline** was planned for the second lesson of three lessons (each lesson was an hour in length). The first lesson was a role-play activity (see *Resource 4* page 48). This was a modified version based upon Culpin and Szuscikiewicz's '*The Era of the Second World War*' Teachers' Guide (Collins). The class was divided into groups of four and each pupil in a group was given a specific character to play. The characters were given names and a little background information about the character. This was an effective activity: it encouraged pupils to recall earlier work and to apply their understanding through the 'filter' of *their* Germany. It pointed up the divergence of views about Hitler within Germany and helped pupils to discuss the topic in a co-operative manner.

> A worthwhile activity in its own right – but here used as a positive **bridge** to the **Lifeline**.

To introduce the **Lifeline** exercise, a sheet with four 'typical' quotations was passed out amongst the class and the pupils were asked to identify which character was most likely to have said which quote. Pupils were asked to remain in character and had to plot their character's emotional reaction – ranging from 'positive', through 'neutral' to 'negative' feelings in relation to key events in German history (see *Resource 3*).

Launching

To launch the activities I began by giving the class clear learning objectives, so that they were aware of why they were performing the tasks in the first place. At the start of the role-play exercise I introduced myself as a waitress working in a café in Munich in 1923 and informed the class of the types of conversation I was able to overhear while doing my job. Although, this may appear slightly bizarre, it did encourage pupils to participate in the activity without embarrassment. After all, if the teacher was prepared to make a fool of herself then why shouldn't they!

> An intriguing role – but one not too dissimilar to assimilating pupil responses prior to the group phase.

To launch the **Lifeline** exercise I persisted with this themed approach. As a result I found that the pupils quickly remembered 'their' character and 'their' context. Quotes from the previous lesson were passed around as a form of recap. Then it was put to the class that it may be possible to stay with the same characters and work out what their reactions would be to events at a later time. In a similar way, they were presently grouped with friends who they may expect to stay friends with all the way through school and beyond.

Instructions

For general instructions, see *Exemplar 1*. From launching to debriefing, pupils needed very little teacher input. At the start of the activity I did stress that answers would not necessarily be right or wrong – and this proved to be an effective form of motivation. The task turned out to be self explanatory in nature, provided that the pupils were aware of how to plot 'their' character's feelings onto the graph, and that they knew what each key event was about. It was helpful to list the events on the board and to take the time to discuss each event in turn before the pupils began to plot their graph. As an alternative,

> The removal of the pressure for consistent 'correct answers' is both liberating and motivating.

depending upon their ability, pupils could be asked to check out these key events from previous work, texts or topic books etc.

Managing the activity

The management of the **Lifeline** went very smoothly for two reasons:

> Firstly, the pupils were given sufficient time to be in character during the role-play activity prior to the **Lifeline** exercise. This provided them with a greater awareness of context, and therefore more confidence to perform.

> Secondly, they were aware that the whole purpose of the activity was a 'different' form of revision. This allowed them to recall factual knowledge they had learnt from previous lessons and make sense of it in a new situation.

The amazing aspect of this whole activity appeared to be that pupils were prepared to think about what they had learnt and question it to a far greater depth than was normally required in other lessons, without having to be led into the activity by the teacher.

Debriefing

Without doubt, the pupils were now able to discuss the key events of the Nazi rise to power with confidence. They had acquired an understanding of why so many people had voted Hitler into power. Issues like censorship, propaganda and education were now being brought out of the framework of the original discussion and were identified as forms of repression. Regardless of their ability, they wanted to find out how propaganda could work, and questioned whether they themselves were actually being conditioned by the same sources in society today. By being in character for over two lessons they appeared to make connections with the feelings they thought 'their' character might experience and what they themselves experienced in their own lives. They could see how these aspects of a totalitarian state would possibly prevent anyone speaking out of turn, and that it was not simply a case of the average German citizen being 'weak' when faced with the apparatus of one 'powerful', cruel individual. From my perspective it appeared that a light had been switched on inside every pupil's head – and they were all finally awake.

Debriefing consisted of a whole-class discussion, which exceeded 40 minutes. To evaluate the exercise I asked the pupils to define in their own words what they thought the term 'dictator' actually meant to them, and how such a person was able to gain and sustain power. This final written task was left open ended. With slight adaptation (ie a writing frame could have been drawn up for the weaker members of the class) it could certainly take the form of a piece of structured extended writing.

Note the degree of flexibility and mid structure according to abilities.

Lifelines can act as a context for useful knowledge recall.

A pleasing indicator.

Many valuable links and connections were apparent, together with pupils' historically apt vocabulary.

That *'so satisfying/oh I get it!'* moment.

Quotations to be handed out

'I'm not bothered as long as I don't have to lug suitcases of money around again.'

'But we should be getting rid of the old order.'

'My dad was a war hero, and for what.'

'But I've been brought up a German all my life.'

Key dates and events

1.	1923	Hyper inflation
2.	1923	Munich Putsch
3.	1924	Dawes Plan
4.	1925	Hitler released from prison
5.	1926	Germany joins the League of Nations
6.	1929	Wall Street Crash
7.	1932	The Enabling Law passed
8.	1933	Many moderates vote for the Nazi Party
9.	1933	Hitler becomes Chancellor
10.	1933	Burning of the Reichstag
11.	1934	Night of the Long Knives
12.	1935	Unemployment falls
13.	1935	Nuremberg rallies
14.	1938	Kristallnacht
15.	1941	The Final Solution

Resource 4   ## Do you support Adolf Hitler? (1923)

It is 1923 in Germany. You and three friends meet in a café. The conversation turns to the Munich Putsch and the trial of Adolf Hitler. You are discussing whether Hitler's ideas are good or bad.

Tasks

1. **In groups of three or four, choose a character each and write an account of what your character might say about Adolf Hitler in the conversation.**

2. **Discuss your character's account with others in the group to see how their opinions differ.**

3. **Write the conversation which may have taken place using all of the characters.**

Mysteries

5 Mysteries

Rationale

Frequently and routinely pupils are given classroom tasks in which they have a page of text or source material and they have only to retrieve the right words from the page to complete the task. There is little challenge, and understanding is not developed to any significant extent. Pupils merely learn how to perform a ritual. This is not how problems and issues present themselves in real life, nor is it higher education. For the activities in this book they will have to take discrete, apparently unconnected pieces of information and fit them together to make sense of disorder, read between the lines, come up with a variety of ideas and evaluate them. The **Mysteries** Strategy mirrors these situations. Fundamental to the activity is the presentation of information in 'semi-digested' form. It is presented on pieces of paper that can be physically manipulated: moving pieces of paper actually helps pupils to think more flexibly.

Students are given 16-25 pieces of information on individual pieces of paper and they produce an answer to a central question *(key question)* or a series of questions. The Strategy is designed, deliberately, to encourage students to deal with ambiguity through addressing a question which has no single correct answer and where they are not even sure what information is relevant – rather like real life in fact. In the process they have to practise and develop some crucial skills:

- interpreting information;
- sorting relevant information from irrelevant;
- classifying;
- making links between disparate pieces of information;
- speculating to form hypotheses;
- checking and refining;
- explaining.

Pupils are encouraged to discuss thoughtful explanations in relation to the central question. Ultimately pupils can be given the opportunity to practice their detailed and discursive writing. Thus they are given an opportunity not only to present evidence in relation to NC Levels, or GCSE objectives, but also to develop the skills they need to improve achievement in relation to those Levels. There is much scope for developing **Mysteries** as a launching pad for well-structured analytical writing, as a number of history educators have endorsed (see Counsell, Byrom, Riley, Wrenn). In particular, Christine Counsell's publications for The Historical Association (1997) and the QCA (1997) are very important in this context.

Key Skills

The 'learning journey' towards solving the problem which a **Mystery** presents depends on co-operative group work in which productive learning and social relationships are fostered. Inevitably disagreement may emerge as group members want to do it their own way. This is particularly true of older and more able students who are more confident of their opinions (even opinionated). If handled sensitively though (and with patience) students can develop communication skills through speaking and listening and learn ways to resolve conflicts.

Presenting pupils with a historical situation with a central dilemma and alternative courses for action, based upon the different motives and values of the key players has long been known to be a powerful means to develop pupils' thinking (see Schemilt, Dickinson, Lee and Ashby). It is an approach to teaching history that has become both popular and well established, witness the plethora of 'Who killed ...?' (Counsell), 'Was King ...?' (Bonham), etc. The *Thinking Through History* **Mysteries** build upon this tradition. By so doing, links to the citizenship requirements can also be built into the learning (see Wrenn) rather than bolted on.

The rationale in *Thinking Through Geography* (Leat, 1998) said '**Mysteries** *are probably the most powerful Strategy in this book – they can completely transform the teaching and learning process*'. Nothing has happened to change this judgement. Indeed the research done since the publication of the geography books (Leat, 1998, and Nichols, 2000) has done much to confirm that view.

Mysteries have a high level of challenge.

Over the past few years the vital historical skills of sorting, selecting, classifying and categorisation have received much attention. **Mysteries** are ideally suited for developing these dispositions.

These represent fundamental higher order, problem-solving skills.

This relates to the Vygotskyan idea of a ZPD (see page 136). Physically doing the task with others may well be important in learning how to do things mentally.

Mysteries access a wide variety of the key skills underpinning the NC, GCSE and AS, A2 specifications.

Negotiated learning through conflict resolutions (this is further developed in the *Community of Enquiry: Philosophy Through History*, see *Chapter 9*).

Such cognitive conflict forces pupils to re-consider their existing understanding of the past.

Mysteries offer a wonderful insight into pupils' ideas – which, in turn, may be used for both diagnostic and formative assessment.

Runaways

Context

This **Mystery** was designed to illustrate the impact which major changes in society can have on the lives of individuals. The investigation incorporates the industrial revolution and the development of the factory system. It was used with a high ability Year 9 group. This group consisted of 32 enthusiastic, well-motivated pupils who are a pleasure to teach and whose quest for further knowledge often results in thought-provoking discussions. This **Mystery** was used in the autumn term of Year 9 in a Unit on the growth of the factory system. The pupils had enjoyed this Unit immensely, as they were introduced to a number of colourful characters. They were also deeply involved with the plight of the children working in the nineteenth-century cotton mills. The group are very able and animated orally. However, I was aware that a number were not fulfilling their true potential in the written form. They were rushing their work and not developing the points which they were making. Many were making unsupported assumptions. I was also aware that this group had developed an intense hatred of a nineteenth-century factory owner. I was hoping to challenge this perception and to stretch their level of understanding of working conditions in a nineteenth-century factory.

In planning the **Mystery** the following learning outcomes were targeted:

- an understanding of the working conditions in a nineteenth-century cotton mill;
- an understanding of the causes for such poor working conditions in a nineteenth-century cotton mill;
- an understanding of the effect which the development of the factory system had upon the urban population of this country in the nineteenth century;
- an ability to recognise that causes are interlinked and are very rarely separate entities;
- to arrive at a historically accurate conclusion.

Preparation

1 I decided upon the *key question* and the issues which we were going to be dealing with. This **Mystery** was based upon a real event which took place in 1820, when a group of young boys absconded from a mill which was owned by Mr A Bradley in Ashbourne, Derbyshire. The names of the boys were fictitiously created, as were their ages, to match those of the Year 9 class.

2 Twenty four statements were prepared relating to the factory system and the industrial revolution. A number of the statements were red herrings and were centred on the personal lives of the boys involved. The statements were cut up and put into envelopes.

3 The class was organised into groups of 4. They had worked in groups before and had done so with maturity and commitment. This class was happy to be put into groups and responded in a way which I had come to expect.

4 The *key question* was put on the board.

Launching

I began the activity by briefly recapping – via a question and answer session – what we had been learning in previous lessons. The pupils were all agreed that the working conditions in a nineteenth-century cotton mill were inhumane and unacceptable. Many were under the assumption that this practice was no longer taking place in the late twentieth century. When I informed them that child labour was indeed still taking place in the world and that a child may have made some of the garments that they were wearing, they went very quiet. I then proceeded to inform them that the aim of the lesson was to investigate who was responsible for the poor working conditions which children of their age had had to endure in the nineteenth century.

Instructions

I organised the groups and distributed the envelopes, but told them not to open them. This class had not attempted a **Mystery** before, but because of the topic they were very enthusiastic to tackle the problem. I asked them for examples of famous detectives. The usual names came up: Agatha Christie, Mulder and Scully etc. We briefly discussed why

Mysteries are good to 'stretch' such pupils both in terms of their efforts and their attitudes.

'Big concepts,' ie **cause and effect** are being re-visited here.

A sense of empathy can thereby be created.

Bridging into the activity from a topical viewpoint, as here, can have a powerful impact.

Another example of
skilled **bridging**, together
with the teacher **modelling**
the task's demands.

these people are successful at their jobs. The conclusion reached was that they all try to solve a mystery by finding clues and evidence. They come up with a possible solution or theory to the mystery and try to prove it using the evidence they have collected.

I proceeded to tell the story of Thomas and John who were both thirteen years of age and worked at a cotton mill in Ashbourne, Derbyshire in 1820. They had run away and had not been seen for several weeks. The boys' parents were very worried, and their employer was very angry. I told the class that they were going to find out why Thomas and John had run away and investigate whether anybody was responsible for the boys taking such drastic action.

I informed the class that the answer they were looking for was hidden amongst the evidence that was inside the envelopes. I also told them that there were a number of red herring cards and they had to be prepared to justify their decision as a group to the class and to explain how they had reached such a conclusion.

I advised the class to read through all the cards in case there were any mistakes on the cards, or in case any group was missing a card. One group was unsure about the definition of *laissez-faire*. Once this was explained, the groups proceeded with the activity.

Managing the activity

The teacher's role is
deliberately that of
facilitator in this group
feedback.

I circulated the room and heard some very encouraging discussions taking place. Five minutes later one group decided that they had found the solution to the **Mystery** of why Thomas and John had run away. They offered the solution I was expecting from them. Using the card '*John was not feeling well that day but his mother still made him go to work at the factory*' the group thought that John's mother was to blame for the boys running away because she had made him go to work. I asked the rest of the class if they agreed. Another group said that they did not agree because when their mother sends them to school they do not run away. For each solution that the class offered, I wrote the detail on the board.

Pupils are encouraged
to offer elaborated and
sustained, oral responses.

I advised the class to try to separate out the cards which were irrelevant and which were not really helping them to answer the question. This took a little longer than I had expected, and as a result I told them that most of the personal information which they had been given about the boys would not help them to solve the **Mystery**. The next solution that was offered was that the factory owner was to blame for the boys running away because the factory owner was making them work too hard and in terrible conditions. The whole class agreed with this point. I then had to take a more central role, and I asked the class in their groups to explain why the factory owner was so strict. They should look at the clues which they had in front of them. Finally, one group suggested that the population was rising and that this population was demanding cloth. The only way the factory owner could keep up with the demand was to make his employees work longer hours. One pupil disagreed with this solution believing that the population could not be blamed because the increasing population was only 'natural'.

Both statements offer
indicators of success.
The former is frequent
in classrooms; the latter
less so.

We were approaching the end of the lesson and the board was a mass of reasons and solutions as to why these two boys had run away from the factory. Some were straightforward simple reasons, others were of a more advanced nature. I addressed each reason in turn and suggested that a number of these reasons were linked together, and that one reason could not be solely responsible. I asked the pupils where I should draw a connecting line between reasons which could be linked together.

Debriefing

Whilst debriefing this task, I asked the pupils what they had learnt from the lesson. One pupil thought that they were made to think. When I asked them what they meant by *think*, they said that they had had to prove their point and to avoid saying the first thing that came into their head, without providing an explanation for their beliefs.

One successful element of this lesson stood out: as a class we had challenged the age-old stereotype of the evil nineteenth-century factory owner.

Follow-up

In order to establish whether or not the pupils had truly been made to *think*, this **Mystery** was followed by their first national curriculum assessment. The task was to produce an extended piece of writing, which would answer the question '*Why were conditions in a* *nineteenth century factory so poor?'* These pupils were more than able to answer a question on how an event happened but not *why* it had happened. The work which they produced was of a very pleasing standard. The pupils were arriving at a decision and using evidence to support the decision which they had made. The work was analytical and accurate; many pupils gained the highest of Levels and were able to display the skill that they had acquired in acknowledging that a number of factors can have an affect on a person's life.

Again, indicators of progress, though a greater confidence in thinking and writing more analytically.

Resource 1   **Task / Mystery Card**

> The year is 1820. Thomas and John are thirteen years of age. The boys both live in Ashbourne, Derbyshire. Thomas and John are best friends and they work in a cotton mill. The cotton mill is owned by Mr A Bradley. Thomas and John have run away and have not been seen for almost two weeks.
>
> Why do you think Thomas and John ran away?
>
> Who do you think was responsible for Thomas and John running away from the factory?

Statements

1. The new machines which had been invented were so heavy that they could only be powered by water or steam.

2. James Hargreaves invented the Spinning Jenny in 1764. Instead of having one spindle like an ordinary spinning wheel, it had 16 or 18. The result of this was that more yarn could be produced at a lower cost.

3. The machines needed more space than there was in the cottage of a handloom weaver. The machines also needed more power than the human arm could provide.

4. Children are very agile. In 1820 they were very useful because it was easy for them to crawl under the machines and repair the broken threads. Although this was dangerous and many children lost limbs, it was a necessary task and that was a part of life working in a factory in the nineteenth century.

5. Factory owners could pay children a lower wage than adult workers.

6. The Government had a laissez-faire attitude towards conditions in the factory system.

7. Britain had a rapidly growing population. This population needed more clothes to wear.

8. In 1801 the population of this country had increased to 8.9 million.

9. Men like Richard Arkwright were building cotton factories. These cotton factories employed men, women and children.

10. The heat in the factory was so unbearable that John had to open the window as he was about to faint.

Continued

Task / Mystery Card (Continued)

11.	John was not feeling well that day but his mother still made him go to work at the factory.

12.	The parents of Thomas and John were very poor and they needed all the money they could get. This is why they sent their children to the factory each day.

13.	In 1750, 80% of people lived in the countryside and worked on farms.

14.	In 1825, 75% of people lived in towns. This is where most of the factories and most of industry was situated. The town was where people could earn the most money.

15.	Laissez-faire means that the Government would not become involved in the problems of the population.

16.	Children were often beaten as a form of punishment – and to make them work harder.

17.	The factory had a horrible smell of gas, mixed with the steam and the unbearable heat.

18.	The heat in some factories was over 90 degrees.

19.	The number of hours children worked in factories was on average over twelve hours each day.

20.	The population was becoming wealthier and with this new money they wanted to buy better quality items.

21.	Overseers had to make sure that the children worked as hard as possible. The more work the children completed, the more money the overseers made. Overseers often used force to make the children work faster.

22.	If a spinner was found with a window open they would have to pay a fine.

23.	Thomas fell asleep while he was working on his machine.

24.	Samuel Crompton invented the Mule, in 1779. The Mule made finer yarn for weaving fine cotton cloth. The Mule had to be used in a large factory.

Bibliography for Mystery Card

Working conditions in a nineteenth-century cotton mill

A D Cameron *Exploring History: Young workers in the Industrial Revolution* (Oliver & Boyd, p14)

Statement 3
R Staton, R Ennion, W Moore. *Three Centuries of Change* (Collins, 1998 p41)

Statement 5
R Staton, R Ennion, W Moore *Three Centuries of Change* (Collins, 1998 p69)

Statement 6
R Staton, R Ennion, W Moore *Three Centuries of Change* (Collins, 1998 p70)

Statement 8
R Staton, R Ennion, W Moore *Three Centuries of Change* (Collins, 1998 p6)

Statement 13
R Staton, R Ennion, W Moore *Three Centuries of Change* (Collins, 1998 p106)

Statement 16
P & M Speed *The Industrial Revolution* (Oxford, p28)

Statement 17
P & M Speed *The Industrial Revolution* (Oxford, p28)

Statement 18
P & M Speed *The Industrial Revolution* (Oxford, p28)

Statement 24
R Staton, R Ennion, W Moore *Three Centuries of Change* (Collins, 1998 p142)

Pit Disaster!

Context

This **Mystery**, based around an investigation into *'Who was responsible for over 200 coal miners' deaths at Hartley in 1862?'* was designed to be used as part of a GCSE scheme of work. In Years 10 and 11, students followed the OCR 'British Social and Economic History' syllabus. This **Mystery** was to be attempted with a Year 10 group of 27 mixed-ability students. Within this group there are individuals who should achieve an A*, and others who might just make the G grade. This group is full of personality, and they thrive on the challenge of a new task. This activity was used in the spring term of Year 10 and we had already completed two of the core topics, which were to be examined. The core topic, which the class was studying at present, was the development of the iron and coal industries. I was aware that they were not finding this to be the most stimulating of topics. More importantly, I was also aware that whilst many students in the class were very able orally, the written work of a number of individuals was of a much lower standard. They faced the familiar problems of not being able to select and recall relevant details to answer the set question, and difficulty in structuring an argument in a logical format.

In planning the **Mystery** the following learning outcomes were targeted:

- to investigate a *key question*, expressed as an investigation;
- to understand the working conditions in a nineteenth century coal mine;
- to understand and appreciate why conditions were so poor in the coalmines;
- to take the opportunity to challenge the opinions of others using the evidence provided;
- to distinguish between what is relevant and what is irrelevant information;
- to identify and classify possible causes of the pit disaster;
- to improve students' ability to make and develop an argument supported with appropriate evidence.

> Absolutely crucial attributes for student success in history, which **Mysteries** are ideally suited to develop.

Preparation

1 Decide upon your *key question*. This **Mystery** is based upon a real event which occurred in the North East coalfield region in 1862. A number of characters within the **Mystery** have been fictitiously created for the purpose of personalising the event and to fit the aims of the exercise.

2 Write the *key question* on the board.

3 Create the appropriate statements. To offer your students every chance of meeting your learning outcomes, both the range and nature of the statements need careful construction. (see *Resource 2*, page 61)

4 Cut the statements up and put them into envelopes – one per group. (see *Resource 2*)

5 I decided against working in large groups, simply because of the number of students in the class who tend to equate 'group work' with the opportunity to do 'no work'. I opted for students working in pairs or in groups of three. I organised the groups in such a way as to allow the more able and conscientious students to aid the less able.

> An example of how a 'local history' dimension may be nested into national history – as the KS3 NC suggests.

> Since 'talk' is so important such 'paired work' is a good alternative. Later on 'pairs' could 'double-up' and 'share' their ideas.

Launching

I began by addressing the issue of where the students thought their weaknesses lay in terms of learning history as a class. It emerged through discussion that the majority found it difficult to structure an extended piece of writing in a successful way. We discussed why this was difficult. I explained that the outcome of the exercise they were about to attempt would help them to answer an extended writing question.

Next, I asked the class if anyone had watched the popular television programme *The X-Files*. This was greeted by a unanimous show of hands. I asked them how Mulder and Scully attempt to investigate the situations that they are faced with every week. They came up with the idea that, in order to solve a crime, evidence has to be found, and information about the victim and the criminal has to be gathered. The most important point to emerge from this discussion was that Mulder and Scully are always trying to convince each other of their different theories and explanations, often by using the same collected evidence. After this initial discussion, I informed the class that they were going

> An interesting way in – by exploring students' difficulties in the first instance.

> An excellent 'bridge' by way of a topical analogy and the analysis of how detectives operate.

to be Mulder and Scully, and that they were going to 'solve' a mystery from the past. It has to be said that the less able pupils appeared to be more concerned over who was going to be Mulder and who was going to be Scully, than the impending task!

Instructions

As this was the first time a **Mystery** had been attempted with this group, clear, precise and explicit instructions were vital.

1 Organise the class into mixed ability groups.
2 Distribute the envelopes but tell the pupils not to open them.
3 Once each group has an envelope, tell them to open the envelope and spread all the statements out on to their desk. Check the number of statements to make sure that each group has a full set.
4 Invite the students to read all of the statements to one another and to make a note of any words or vocabulary that they do not understand.
5 Ask pupils to separate out the largest card, which has the *key question* on. (For easy reference this card was orange)
6 Ask a student to read this **Mystery** card (see *Resource 2*). Explain to them exactly what the problem is, and the **Mystery** which they have to try to solve. In this instance the **Mystery** card contained some personal information about the Armstrong family and how they were affected by a local mining disaster in 1862 at New Hartley Colliery in Northumberland.
7 The *key question* the pupils had to answer was: *'What exactly happened on 16th January 1862, and who do you think was responsible for the accident?'*
8 Re-emphasise that in their small groups, and by using the cards, they are to try to answer the mystery – by talking, arguing and reasoning – using evidence from the statements.
9 Explain that some of the statements will be useless in answering the question, and they should not be afraid to discard any irrelevant information.
10 Suggest that by physically moving the **Mystery** statement cards around, new ideas may well develop which could help them to organise their information.

> Easily manipulated statements and historical understanding.

Managing the activity

The first suggestion I offered to the class was that they should decide which causes or cards were relevant to the question and which were not, and to divide the cards into two piles. They managed to do this very quickly – but all the groups wanted me to check their work. This was a clear illustration to me of the lack of confidence which these pupils have in their own ability. I managed to convince them of their own convictions and asked one group to offer the rest of the class an explanation of one card which they believed was relevant and one card which was irrelevant. The rest of the class either expressed agreement or not. Whilst this process was taking place in the group phase, I tried to avoid the temptation of interfering and directing the lesson. Only when it was absolutely necessary would I ask: *'Are you sure that this is relevant?'* A lot of groups believed in the first place that all the cards containing personal information were relevant.

Once this task was complete, and I was satisfied with the process which had taken place, we moved on to the next activity. The next activity was to organise and re-classify all the relevant statements according to their social, economic and political nature. The pupils were familiar with such terms, but a brief recap was given for the benefit of the weaker pupils.

Next, the students had to tackle the issue of: *'Which statements were <u>direct causes</u>, and which statements were <u>indirect</u> causes of the New Hartley pit disaster of 1862?'* Before we attempted this difficult yet essential task, I discussed with the class what the definition of direct and indirect causes was. I used a modern analogy to ensure that the pupils fully understood this concept. The recent demise in the status of Newcastle United Football Club was an obvious choice. I asked why the club was struggling to achieve success when only a few years ago they were a powerful and formidable football team. The students' enthusiasm was predictable and they offered various causes, which were written on the blackboard. We then decided that the *direct* causes were that the team was inconsistent: they could not score goals, and they were conceding too many goals. The *indirect* causes began with the departure of the inspirational manager, Kevin Keegan. Added to this was the selling

> Through deploying a recent analogy, the seeds of **bridging/transfer** may be sown.

of high quality players, a new chairman, and the dissatisfaction of the fans.

Once the students were on task, I circulated around the class listening out for any thought-provoking discussions taking place. I stopped the class and asked a group to explain to the rest of the class the decisions which they had arrived at. Instead of directing the lesson myself, the pupils were in charge.

> You want the pupils to do some of the initiating.

Finally, the pupils were asked: *'Can you offer a valid explanation as to why the disaster at New Hartley Colliery happened in 1862?'* I proceeded to ask for volunteers from the groups to offer their answers. One pupil offered his explanation: *'There was only one shaft at New Hartley Colliery so this was why the men died, because they could not be rescued.'* I asked: *'So, whose fault was this?'* He said: *'It was the colliery owner's fault.'* I challenged this by asking: *'Who is responsible for overseeing the maintenance of health and safety within the work place?'* Eventually several pupils came up with: *'The Government.'* I then pointed them towards the statement *'In 1872 the Coalmine Regulation Bill became Law'*. This Act included the provision that two air outlets must be provided at every mine. With this knowledge, the class moved more towards the view that perhaps the Government and their laissez-faire attitude was in part responsible for the poor working conditions inside the mine, leading to the disaster.

> Here the pupils are offering a substantiated explanation, based upon their own version of events.

One of the most encouraging aspects of this exercise was watching my Year 10 pupils, who had in the past displayed little interest in mining, arguing and contributing to a thoughtful and provoking discussion over an incident involving a nineteenth-century coal mine.

Debriefing

The process of debriefing this exercise began as soon as I was aware that a number of groups were arriving at a decision as to what happened on 16th January 1862 and who was responsible. One group suggested that: *'It was Jack's father's fault because he was ill and this meant that Jack's family had to go to work in the colliery. If John Armstrong had not been ill then Jack would not have been working down the mine'.* Immediately another pupil responded with: *'That's shocking, you can't blame his Dad!'* By circulating the room whilst the pupils were dealing with the exercise I was aware which groups had reached a higher level of understanding and so encouraged them to offer their explanation to the rest of the class and to explain the process they used in arriving at a decision. I also encouraged other groups to offer their explanation if it was different from the previous group's. By using this method an enthusiastic discussion evolved.

> This has to be regarded as a success in terms of student motivation and engagement.

As part of the debriefing I asked the pupils what they had learnt from the lesson. Instead of asking for oral contributions, I asked the pupils if they would write down what they thought they had gained. From this, the pupils' improved grasp of key vocabulary was evident. Other responses reflected the variety of learning outcomes outlined earlier. Overall the pupils thought this exercise had helped them to understand that a mass of irrelevant data does not gain extra marks, nor does it answer a specific question. The pupils had learnt – as Counsell's ideas suggest (1997) – that the most effective way of dealing with an extended piece of writing is to decide which information is 'question relevant' in its importance, and to avoid 'padding out' their writing with irrelevant narrative. In addition, to be most successful, they must develop their argument by selecting out 'big points' and by supporting these with appropriate 'little points', therefore making conclusions by using the relevant information from their explanations.

> A most worthwhile insight into student thinking, or **metacognition**, in action.

Follow-up

In order to establish exactly what had been learnt from this **Mystery**, the pupils were set the task of answering an essay question based upon conditions in nineteenth-century coalmines. I set this task for homework to be completed over the Easter holidays. Considering that a period of about two weeks had elapsed since the pupils completed the **Mystery**, the results were very encouraging. The vast majority of pupils had answered the question, using precise and discursive language. The most satisfying part of this exercise was receiving a piece of work from a pupil who in the past had always submitted their homework late and had struggled to construct a paragraph. On this occasion, the pupil submitted an extended piece of quality writing in which the question had been answered analytically supported by the relevant narrative.

Adapting the Strategy

I had initially thought about using a thinking plan with each group, along similar lines to a writing frame. This would have spoon-fed the class as to which activity they had to do next, and so on. After consulting my head of department I decided against this because I felt that it would interfere with the flow of the lesson, and would become far too prescriptive. Upon reflection one or two groups may have benefited from this, particularly those with the most disruptive pupils. They had found it difficult to remember the instructions given to them only five minutes earlier.

Task / Mystery Card

John and Mary Armstrong live in New Hartley, Northumberland. John, Mary and their five children all work in New Hartley Colliery. On 16th January 1862, their son Jack, aged 15, was killed while he was working in the mine. Jack was a thruster and had lost his life when the steam engine's beam crashed and fell over the mineshaft. John and Mary are heartbroken over their loss.

What exactly happened on 16th January 1862 and who do you think was responsible for the accident?

Statements

1. In the second half of the eighteenth century a wide range of industries needed heat, for processes such as brick making and brewing. These industries were all stimulated by the growing population.

2. In 1824, George Stephenson built the Liverpool to Manchester railway. This railway needed coal for the engines.

3. In 1761, the Duke of Bridgewater and James Brindley completed their canal. Bridgewater was the father of canal building in Great Britain and he was also the proprietor of several coalmines.

4. In 1700, 2.9 million tons of coal was produced and consumed.

5. Abraham Darby took over the Coalbrookdale Iron Works in 1793. He built six new blast furnaces and bought all the local coalmines. The demand for iron was growing, and as a result the demand for coal was also increasing.

6. By 1830, 45 million tons of coal was being produced and consumed.

7. In 1815, Sir Humphrey Davy designed the miners' safety lamp. It had a flame, which was surrounded by wire gauze. If dangerous gases were present the colour of the flame would change.

8. Coal was used for heating in homes and for washing and cooking.

9. On 16th January 1862, the miners had forgotten to take the canary cage down the mineshaft.

10. In 1821, there were one million homes in Great Britain, but by 1851 there were two and a quarter million. These homes desperately needed coal for cooking, washing and heating.

Continued

Resource 2   **Task / Mystery Card** *(Continued)*

11. One by one the bodies were lifted to the surface and laid side by side for their relatives to identify them. 204 miners had lost their lives.

12. Jack had been at work for eight hours without anything to eat or without any fresh air.

13. News of the tragedy spread fast and Queen Victoria asked about the miners' chances and expressed her hope for their lives.

14. From Friday January 16th to Wednesday January 21st the men had been trapped without food or air.

15. Jack Armstrong was extremely tired as he had been at work since 6 o'clock in the morning. Jack kept falling asleep inside the colliery.

16. Jack's father had been ill for several weeks and was unable to work. His mother and all the children had to go to work or the family would starve.

17. Jack's friend Harry was normally the thruster, but he was at home because of illness. Jack had to do his job.

18. In 1862, the Coalmines Regulation Bill became law. This Act included the provision that two air outlets must be provided at every mine.

19. There was only one shaft at New Hartley Colliery. If the men that were trapped were to be saved they would have to come up the shaft that the broken beam had fallen down. There was no other way to rescue them.

20. In 1840, the Government set up an enquiry into conditions in the coalmines. The results were published in 1842, and deeply shocked the middle class. The Mines Act was passed in 1842: it was now illegal for women and children under the age of 10 to be employed underground in the mines.

21. The owner of New Hartley Colliery was convinced that the Davy lamp kept miners safe, so he sent them deeper underground.

22. Canaries in cages were taken down into the mine. If a deadly gas escaped, the canary quickly died, and so the miners would know they needed to get away from the area.

Bibliography for Mystery Card

New Hartley Colliery disaster

Statement 1
B Walsh *British Social and Economic History* (John Murray, 1997 p112)

Statement 3
B Walsh *British Social and Economic History* (John Murray, 1997 p142)

Statement 4
B Walsh *British Social and Economic History* (John Murray, 1997 p112)

Statement 5
B Walsh *British Social and Economic History* (John Murray, 1997 p103)

Statement 6
B Walsh *British Social and Economic History* (John Murray, 1997 p112)

Statement 7
B Walsh *British Social and Economic History* (John Murray, 1997 p117)

Statement 10
B Walsh *British Social and Economic History* (John Murray, 1997 p177)

Statement 18
R Staton, R Ennion, W Moore *Three Centuries of Change* (Collins, 1998 p60)

Statement 20
R Staton, R Ennion, W Moore *Three Centuries of Change* (Collins, 1998 p72)

Wilf's War

Context

The aim of this **Mystery** is to commence an enquiry into the path of one local individual through World War I. This provides an in-depth study, which will satisfy the NC Orders. By personalising the impact of war on a specific individual it is hoped that pupils will hold a deeper and greater understanding of the events and the effects of conflict. The enquiry is set locally, which adds to pupils' interest. It could easily be altered to fit any other individual in a local context. This enquiry is the pupils' first introduction to Wilf. Our department is now intending to incorporate *Wilf's War* into our Year 9 Schemes of Work. Following the **Mystery**, pupils will follow the course of *Wilf's War* through the following aspects:

- training;
- journey to the front;
- experience of the trenches;
- into battle;
- Wilf at the Sornme;
- Wilf is wounded;
- recuperation and regeneration;
- Wilf's final battle!

The aim of the **Mystery** is:

- to raise pupils' awareness of the multitude of reasons why soldiers volunteered in the early days of the War;
- to build a personal identity for Wilf.

Preparation

I began the lesson by writing on the blackboard four phrases which I hoped the pupils would recognise:

Poppy Day
War Memorial
Roll of Honour
Remembrance Day

Next I asked: '*What event might link them together?*' To develop the questioning, you could pose questions relating to the casualties' names on the local War Memorial. Finally, I posed the open question to the pupils: '*Given the high chance of being killed in a war, would you – today – choose to join an army?*' Their responses were – predictably – wide ranging. Before commencing the **Mystery**, the key point to be reached is to establish that attitudes to joining up to the army and 'doing your bit' for King and country which prevailed at the start of World War I were very different from today.

The class should be divided into groups of 3 or 4. Groups should be of similar ability levels. Each group will be given an envelope of clues. It would be possible to differentiate the clues, where necessary or desirable, by decreasing the number given to a group. In practice, I have found that all pupils will be able to come up with some ideas from the clues with a minimum of help.

Launching

Pupils are given the *key question* to drive the **Mystery** forward: '*Why did Wilf Smith join the Durham Light Infantry (the DLI)?*' The only other instruction needed is to suggest that pupils should look for a number of reasons. Leave things deliberately vague. Pupils can sort the clues in whatever classification they find suitable. No time limit need be given at this stage.

Managing the activity

In my experience, pupils soon get to grips with sorting the clues and come up with some interesting variations of categories. If there is little headway perhaps the help could be given '*What groups could we put the clues into to help you understand*'. No mention should be made of red herrings at this stage.

The sorting of clues should take around 10 to 15 minutes. Pupils can either list the reasons on paper or use the key clues as a reminder. My general thoughts are that pupils should be left to think through their strategies.

Follow-up

Oral feedback from groups is a starting point. In this situation it is often good practice to bring other pupils in to make points and expand explanations without too much teacher-led input. Let the pupils lead the discussions! The teacher can bring together responses in a spider chart on the board.

A range of valuable alternative activities for pupils to 'cash-in' and apply their previous thinking.

Task 1 Once a list of reasons is resolved from the group, pupils can attempt the *20 point strategy*. Each group has 20 points, which they must distribute in proportion to the reasons they think are most important, eg 'peer pressure'=8 points, 'propaganda'=4 points etc, up to 20 in total. This produces a ranking which is evaluative.

Task 2 a Why did Wilf decide to join up?

  (If a class might struggle with this:

  group together all the statements about Wilf's family;

  group together all the statements about money;

  group together all the statements about height;

  group together all the statements about Wilf's friends.)

  b What would Wilf have said about why he had signed up?

  c Who might have tried to persuade him not to sign up?

  d What reasons might they have used?

  e What assumptions have you used in relation to Task 1? (a much more advanced task, but it starts to unpack issues about reasoning)

  f Draw a map of your explanation for Task 1. (This is a task which helps to turn thinking into writing. In early stages it has to be modelled on the blackboard with pupils' help. This would include giving groups of items a name, annotating the importance or role of the group in the explanation (eg, main reason), and drawing lines between groups to show connection and sequence within the writing, etc.

Task 3 A good homework, or individual follow-up, is to use a GCSE format question. For example, the famous Kitchener recruitment poster and a question worth 8 marks: '*Does the use of propaganda posters such as … fully explain why young men 'joined up' so eagerly in 1914?*'

Debriefing

Ideally, this should be done immediately after the **Mystery**. The pupils must synthesise the process. This is the most difficult part of the exercise from the teacher's point of view. The following gives some ideas:

- How well did the pupils work together?
- How did they sort out the clues?
- What were the main categories – the 'big ideas'?
- What about the red herrings?
- What skills have pupils used? – generally very complex.
- When have pupils used these same skills before?
- Where else could they be used?

Adapting the Strategy

Start the next lesson with a 2 minute recap. Ask all the pupils to list the reasons why Wilf joined up. You will be surprised at the level of recall. Build on the knowledge of Wilf's background as he goes on to training and sets off for France. Wilf's War has begun!

Resource 3   **Mystery Card**

In 1914 Wilf was 17 years old.	A private in the DLI got one shilling per day (5 pence).
He had lived in the same house in Stanley all his life with his parents and two sisters.	There were a lot of 'Kitchener' posters in Stanley in 1914.
Wilf worked on a farm outside Stanley, County Durham.	Wilf paid his mother 2/4d a week (12 pence).
Wilf wanted to be a footballer, but he was too small.	Maisie, Wilf's 19 year-old sister was planning to get married.
Wilf had a girlfriend, Agnes. Other lads thought she was very pretty.	Tommy told Wilf that the 19th Battalion was stationed in Gateshead.
Wilf was an excellent swimmer.	Wilf was poor at reading and writing.
In 1913 Agnes got a job as a 'live-in' servant for a 'posh' house in Newcastle.	Wilf was paid 3 shillings a week (15 pence).
The 19th Battalion of the DLI were called the 'bantams' for men under 5ft 3ins tall.	During the war Wilf wrote many letters home.
Wilf's mother had wanted more children, especially boys.	Agnes had been considered clever at school.
A picture of Edward VII was hung on the wall over the mantelpiece in Wilf's house.	The furthest Wilf had ever travelled was to see Newcastle United (at home) with Tommy. He had to save up to do this.
The son of Agnes's employer had signed up to be an officer instead of going to Cambridge University.	Wilf's father had fought in the Boer War. He had caught TB and never worked after he came home.
Wilf's home was a crowded 'two up and two down' in Stanley.	Tommy Fishburn boasted that he was the first soldier to 'sign up' in Stanley.
Wilf was only 5ft 2ins tall.	Wilf looked after the horses on the farm.

6 Reading Photographs and Pictures

6 Reading Photographs and Pictures

Rationale

Modern history textbooks are full of photographs and illustrations. Too often, though, pictures are placed within the text simply for illustration, to create a visual image of a well-known person, an invention, or a historic event. They run the risk of being underused or even ignored. Clearly, there is insufficient time to de-construct every visual source using the necessary evidential skills. Within history, more practice is required, however, to develop pupils' range of visual literacy skills – including inference, reliability, validity, utility and significance.

There can be little doubt that visual literacy, in the broadest sense, is required in the twenty first century. We live in a highly visual society, saturated with television, cinema, billboard and magazine images, and we owe it to students to help them decode the information in these media. And, at a much more practical level, there are real advantages in being able to read photographs in the pursuit of higher achievement. GCSE and A Level examination papers use photographs, pictures and paintings extensively and many pupils miss marks by not using the information that is readily available within them.

However, we give little explicit attention to the skills embedded in the process. As with so much in education we expect it to happen by 'osmosis' – it permeates the curriculum – which usually means that it does not happen at all. There is an explicit reference to photographs in the statutory Order for history:

> *'Historical enquiry:*
>
> *Pupils should be taught to:*
> *1. identify, select and use…*
> *i. the media… pictures… photographs…*
> *2. evaluate the sources used, select and record…'*

(DfEE, 1999)

There are three rich seams to exploit in visual images:

- Firstly (and obviously), we want pupils to look more carefully and to see more of what is there – to **scan** rather than **skim**.
- Secondly, we want pupils to go beyond what they can see and make connections between what is visible and what they already know. The de-construction of visual images helps develop important **enquiry skills** through questioning structures, as recently recognised through 'levels of inference' picture frames.
- Finally, we want pupils to start **speculating** and **hypothesising** from the evidence in the photograph. This would imply questions such as *'What happened prior to the instant of the click of the shutter?' 'What happened after?' 'Why were those people there?'* and *'How did this place come to be like this anyway?'* Or *'Why did the artist paint this scene? What ideas lay behind the composition?'* and *'How much of this was a product of the world the artist inhabited?'* These matters of 'witting' and 'unwitting' testimony are the stuff of **higher order** historical Thinking Skills. This is the essence of the enquiry process.

The Exemplars included in this Chapter are designed to encourage pupils to develop their ability to do all three.

It should also be recognised that the use of visual images is a major vehicle in differentiation. Pupils are not required to read text, therefore in many ways some of the barriers to accessing understanding are removed. Through using photographs or pictures you begin to unlock some of the talent unused in low-achieving pupils, and in the process you boost their self-esteem.

Jews in Germany

Context

This activity was carried out with a Year 9 mixed ability group. It was designed to help develop a variety of evidence skills. It is a good Strategy for getting students to think about interpretations of evidence, and to be critical of the evidence they are presented with.

Through this visual activity pupils are able to access knowledge and develop new ways of learning. I find visual images particularly useful when dealing with a sensitive topic such as the Holocaust: to fully appreciate the horrors of it, one must see carefully selected visual images. Such images tend to be embedded in the long-term memory for much longer than other media.

Before we look at the Holocaust we spent time examining life in Germany from both the Jewish, and the non-Jewish German perspective. I used clips of the BBC TV *'Peoples' Century'* (*'The Master Race'*) video, which clearly points out how the treatment of the Jews progressively worsened, and how Goebbels used propaganda. (If you can't get hold of this video, then a simple discussion will suffice)

Whenever I start work on the Holocaust, students always ask me: *'Why did so many Germans do nothing to stop what Hitler was doing?'* You may like to use two other Thinking Skills Strategies within the book which address similar issues: the **Lifeline** *Exemplar 3: The Rise of Hitler* (see page 45) and the **Community of Enquiry** *Exemplar 2: 38 Witnesses* (see page 124). We had previously discussed Germany's economic prosperity, and how Hitler effectively used propaganda so that people would not be aware of, or, more importantly, would not believe – or want to believe – what was happening to the Jews. And that Hitler was able to rule by fear. However, some pupils still fail to see how this combination could have such consequences and enabled the Holocaust to happen. I find presenting students with a limited selection of photos and asking them to base a decision on them, helps them to appreciate more fully the role of propaganda and how evidence is often based on interpretation.

> Once again, pupils are being invited to apply their existing knowledge base.

> Key vocabulary is reinforced.

Preparation

Although this lesson may at first appear ambitious, I have found it to be a good way of encouraging class debate and getting pupils to see things from a different perspective. So don't be daunted.

Pupils are asked to examine and interpret the photos and then explain: *'What kind of life would you have had – if you were either a German or a Jew?'* It was suggested that the pupils should select from a series of photos. Finding suitable photos for this purpose was easy. There are so many available in a variety of books (or from the Internet), eg IWM, SHP, PRO – you won't have to look far. Select photos that photocopy well and provide each pair of pupils with a set.

> Selecting appropriate evidence in order to argue a position is worthwhile.

Pupils were initially set to work in pairs, but later in fours. It may be advisable to give some thought to how to construct the fours in the classroom. You will also need to number the pairs either Number 1 or Number 2. Since I was working with a mixed ability group I put some thought into this arrangement.

Launching

I started the lesson by quizzing the pupils about their knowledge of a topical event: the Louise Woodward baby-battering trial, which was taking place in the USA at the time. I asked *'Why had people already made up their minds about whether she was guilty, or not, even before hearing the evidence?'* Also, *'Why did so many people seem to have such fundamentally different views?'* This worked well and the ensuing discussion delivered a variety of starting points: *'It depends on which television station or newspaper you read, you are given snippets of information and not the whole picture'*, *'people are biased, because of their nationality or race'* and one less able boy simply said *'people believe what they want to and refuse to look at the alternatives'*. We had a quick re-cap about how you read pictures, ie why is the background of a photo important? why was the photo taken? By now I felt the students were ready.

> Any topical event – such as this – forms a useful **bridge**, or can act as a 'spark' for good connections.

> Careful **scaffolding** helps pupils create meaning through talk, followed next, by an achievable diagrammatic task.

Instructions

I put on the blackboard the questions we were hoping to answer by the end of the lesson:

1 What was life like in Germany for the Jews during Hitler's rule?
2 What was life like in Germany under Hitler, and how might this help explain why the Holocaust was able to happen?

> Evidence here of mostly open questions from the teacher designed to illicit a range of alternative responses.

Students were put into pairs. I then divided the class so that half of the class were answering one question and the other half were answering the other question. (Number 1 groups and Number 2 groups)

Number 1 groups were given a series of photos showing what life was like for the Jews. They were asked to sequence the photos in a roughly chronological framework. In order to do this, pupils need to be given photos which clearly fit into themes, eg early Nazi measures (burning books), through to the Nuremberg Laws and what they stood for, to Kristallnact, the ghettoes and the concentration camps, and the death camps. Number 2 groups, who were examining aspects of life in Germany which might help explain why the Holocaust happened, needed photos which cover issues of relative economic prosperity, propaganda, racist policies and fear.

> Visual images can act as a 'springboard' to disciplined imagination.

Once the groups have placed the photos in a chronological or themed framework they should study the photos and use them to jot down ideas about the events of the Holocaust, ie storyboard their ideas. This gives them a clear framework for the final activity, a piece of extended writing. Each picture will give a good starting point, but do remember to emphasise that they are to use *these selected images* to form their interpretation of what life was like in Germany.

Managing the activity

Pupils were given 20 minutes to either sequence the events or put them into themes and then jot down some ideas.

Initially, a few pupils were concerned that they had not got the chronological order completely correct, but I made it clear that I simply wanted a rough framework. Feeling happier that there were no strict right or wrong answers, pupils worked on the task much better than I had expected. I suspect that pairing a stronger pupil with a less able one had something to do with this. Within the mixed-ability context, some students did finish earlier than others, so I got them to start storyboarding their ideas. Pupils had done this before so they understood what was meant, but it may help to explain at the start of the lesson what you eventually want them to do with their noted ideas.

Once they had done this, the pairs had to join up to make groups of four, and explain their findings. Pupils were only given a few minutes to discuss this, as I did not want them to slip off task. We had set out to try to understand two different perspectives of life in Germany based on thinking about the evidence we are presented with, so class discussion now focused on this.

Debriefing

I started by asking: *'What was life like for the Jews?'* Through the use of the photos pupils were able to give a very full answer. I then posed a question to the Number 2 groups: *'After all the awful things they had just heard, how could they possibly try to explain why German people allowed this to happen?'* The pupils were only allowed to use the evidence they had been given. I wanted Number 2 groups only to answer this, since they had examined the relevant evidence.

Although a little out of context the following comments and thoughts arose during the lesson:

Pupil 1 *Well if you were a German, life was quite good. People had holidays and better food. In the pictures people also seem happy. So they would probably not want to believe that Hitler was a bad person seeing as he was good to a lot of people.*

Me *Any other reasons from what you've seen as to why lots of people did nothing to stop him?*

Pupil 2 *The fear of the SS men and what they might do to you.*

Me *But if you knew what's happening to the Jews would you be prepared to do nothing?*

Pupil 3 *Yes if I was going to get shot.* (a few titters followed)

Me *So you'd think only of yourself?*

There was a short silence and I started to think they had missed the point – of using selected evidence to sustain an explanation – but next, things have improved...

Pupil 1 *But would we really know what life was like for the Jews?*

Pupil 2 *Of course, you would have seen the Jews being taken away.*

Pupil 1 *Yes but would we know where they were going? Because from our evidence, Hitler is a good person who gives us jobs. Would we think he could do anything really bad?*

Pupil 4 *I wouldn't believe him cos you'd be stupid to...*

Pupil 3 *Or maybe too frightened too...*

Time to recap, and push a little further I thought.

Me *So then, from the evidence you have, Hitler shows up very well, and you may not want to believe the stories if your life is good. But remember I only gave you a small amount of evidence. Surely people there at the time would have seen the truth in their everyday lives?*

Pupil 5 *But more evidence might have made us believe Hitler more, or fear him more. Not everybody would have believed the propaganda but many people would have been scared.*

So now I asked: *What was life like in Germany during Hitler's rule?*

Pupil 1 *People had different experiences so it would depend who you were. Some Germans would believe the propaganda and so believe Hitler was a good man winning the war.*

Me *How much of what you have seen is true? Would all Germans have had this experience? Would they all believe the propaganda, or might they want to turn a blind eye?*

I asked the pupils how photographs had helped their understanding of life in Germany. Many agreed that because they had seen the visual images, it made it easier to remember things but also easier to use their imagination, as the photos gave them a starting point. Apart from the obvious fact that I couldn't give them all the possible photos, I asked if they could explain why I had given them a particular selection. Some pupils were unable to appreciate that I was trying to make them see things in a certain way, while others could see that, like them, people in Germany would also have had access to only a selected amount of information.

Within my planning I had not fully appreciated the role of class discussion and the potential benefits of peer tutoring. It was, without doubt, through the discussion part of the lesson that the more able pupils were able to assist the less able to appreciate what they had learnt. Through discussion the pupils were more able to understand those people who saw the Jews being taken away and did nothing through fear. They were more able to understand that this fear, together with the selected information given, may have stopped people from doing anything to help, and that this did not necessarily make them a 'bad' person given the context of the situation.

> An interesting distinction, revealing a range of historical awareness and understanding amongst the pupils.

Follow-up

Having suggested to the pupils that not all German citizens would have believed the propaganda, or turned a blind eye to the Final Solution, our follow-up lesson focused on Nazi resistance groups, such as 'The White Rose group', and the roles of 'registers' and 'rescuers', such as Oskar Schindler and Raoul Wallenberg.

Resource 1

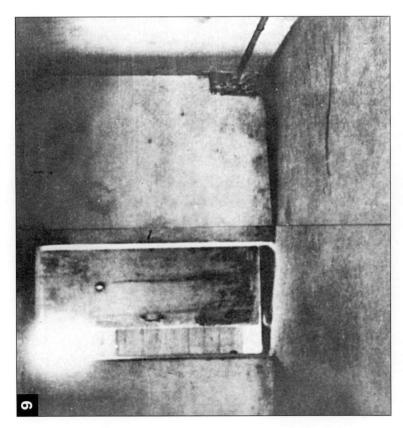

Sources of photographs

The photos I used were from the following textbooks:

Smoke and Ashes: the Story of the Holocaust (Barbara Rogasky), and *Germany* (Robert Gibson & Jon Nichol).

Jewish (Number 1 group)
(from *Smoke and Ashes*, see above)

1 Burning books of 'un-German spirit'

2 Kristallnact

3 Synagogues burnt

4 Jews forced to scrub the streets

5 Old Jewish woman being tormented

6 Jews forced to dig their own graves

7 SS men separating the men and women
   and selecting the healthy

8 Life in the Camps

9 A gas chamber

Germany (Number 2 group)
(from *Germany*, see above)

10 Mass rallies

11 Opening of the new autobahn

12 Youth group celebrations

13 Hitler digging for the new autobahn

14 Hitler with some children

Exemplar 2

The Home Front in World War Two

Context

This Exemplar was designed as an introductory activity for Year 12 students who were beginning to come to grips with the demands of A Level. The objectives of the lesson are:

- to develop the concept of **interpretation**;
- to foster an appreciation of the **complexity** of historical sources and the inherent problems contained within them;
- to raise awareness of the value of **cognitive skills** in history;
- to promote awareness that photographs are not neutral recordings of an objective truth.

> Sophisticated visual literacy is a pre-requisite for the more advanced, anlaytical and interpretative demands required within the AS and A2 specifications.

As is normally the case at A Level, the students were in mixed ability groups to encourage them to learn from each other. The students were used to group discussions and problem-solving exercises using primary sources. The previous week they had been given a skills exercise using nineteenth century maps which required them to categorise sources in order to come up with themes for discussion such as trade, settlement and transport routes. Members of the group are developing enquiry skills, which will culminate in the production of a personal study for the coursework component of their course. The hope is that Thinking Skills will help to drive this process forward, whilst at the same time promoting history as an exciting and enjoyable subject.

> Visual discursive strategies can address the issue of transition and consequent loss of self-esteem experienced by many 16 year old students upon entering Year 12.

Preparation

The primary resource is the set of black and white photographs (see *Resource 2*). Once photocopied, the photographs need to be cut out to produce 14 separate images. Each group should have their own set, together with a Task Sheet and some writing paper. Laminating the master copies proved to be a good idea!

> This Strategy is readily transferable to any historical topic or event.

If you wish to try the launching idea as outlined below you will also need some current photographs on a topical issue from a recent newspaper or from your local area.

Launching

With an A Level class it should be possible to discuss the meaning of **Reading Photographs** and tease from them the point that photographs must be challenged and analysed carefully due to inherent properties such as prejudice, bias, motive, intended audience etc. This helps to get them thinking!

I then did a quick exercise on the board to stimulate the students into thinking about themes in history and links between themes. At this point you could use some photographs from a newspaper, your local area or some other visual primary sources which the students are already familiar with. In this instance it was useful to refer back to the previous lesson on nineteenth century maps to provide a conceptual reference point.

> Once again, note the value of **bridging** from the topical, and known, student experience.

The students were shown three enlarged photographs taken on Newcastle quayside depicting features which had been drawn on the nineteenth century maps: a warehouse, an industrial site and a residential area. When questioned, the students were able to spot more complex links such as: a residential area suggests local employment which links to healthy trade and the existence of an industrial site. As a bridging exercise this served the purpose of making the students aware of how they could transfer their learning about maps to photographs.

This took approximately 10 minutes. Though the class was keen to discuss further links they had to be firmly steered onto the first main activity.

Instructions

The *Task Sheet* takes the place of much specific instruction. The following pointers may be useful for *Task 1*. To begin with you may need to run through a simple example to give them confidence. Warn the students that they should only fill in the boxes when the group is in agreement. The most obvious groupings are: evacuation, resilience to war, and preventative measures. When the students are stretched further, some other possibilities are: family life, employment, safety, leisure time, social effects, economic effects, occupational effects. *Column C* may need teacher support.

Thinking Through History

For *Task 2* groups may suggest that from photograph number 3, for instance, the historian cannot be sure that this is a training exercise. As a result they may come up with a caption such as 'A German male spy dressed up as a woman attempts to cross a road block'.

Managing the activity

The Year 12 students involved in this activity were very familiar with group work. They were well motivated and enjoyed progressing through the range of tasks. Some groups went off at tangents. The metacognition tasks proved to be more difficult, and while they did rise to the challenge, a couple of groups needed to be guided and supported in order to verbalise thinking processes. In order to help them with this, I suggested they should reflect upon their discussions whilst on a particular task.

Debriefing

While students did find it highly challenging to analyse their own thinking, by the end of the lesson they were in full agreement that the experience had improved their understanding of how they learned, using photographs as historical sources and their ability to work as part of a team. The *Task Sheet* proved a little over-ambitious for a single lesson. Once warmed up, the groups became so engaged in the tasks that it seemed a shame to interrupt them mid-flow. With hindsight I realised that the completion of all the tasks is not the most important thing: rather, it is the thinking processes which the students employ that are important. The *Tasks* should therefore be used selectively, depending upon the ability, enthusiasm and responsiveness of the students.

Within each group the students adopted different roles and responded well to mini-deadlines that were used to move them through *Tasks 1 and 2*. *Recording Grid 1* for *Task 1* produced some expected responses, such as evacuation, resilience to war, and morale. *Recording Grid 2*, however, provoked much more powerful thinking - and some students even entered into animated discussions about their categories. One student remarked *'Look! You all need to think much more deeply – I suggest internal and external propaganda as our themes.'* Another group considered chronological grouping such as 'before, during and after' the War. This led to an interesting discussion about the problems of dating and how deceptive photographs can be.

Once the students had completed *Recording Grid 1* they were anxious to give me their conclusions for *Columns C* and *D*. The launching exercise had clearly helped them with *Column C*. For *Column D*, when asked how they had arrived at their themes, one student noted that for social history it helped to empathise with people in the past, and that this line of thought had produced themes such as family life and leisure time. A particularly able student suggested that: *'initially people categorise images visually by grouping together similar images such as children, for the theme of evacuation. The next stage'*, he went on, *'is to look for inter-relationships within the images'*. When asked how these inter-relationships would be arrived at, another student replied *'by using background knowledge and an understanding of processes'*. This was the high point in the lesson and subsequently encouraged other students to verbalise their own cognitive skills and inclinations.

An example of metacognitive talk.

In *Task 2* students coped well with the methodology of using photographs. Discussions between the students led to an appreciation that some aspects of human behaviour are inherently inaccessible to the camera, and that the act of taking a photograph alters the conduct of those who know they are being observed.

To conclude the lesson, the groups of students were asked to brainstorm what they thought the benefits of the lesson had been. One group thought that deconstructing photographs had helped them fully to appreciate some of the inherent problems in using such sources. Another group started discussing a different lesson in which they had needed to categorise information in history. With a little prompting, they were then able to talk about the transferable nature of the skills they had been using. Links were also made with glaciation processes in geography, and acids and bases in chemistry. A 'bridging' remark was also made concerning the fact that photographs and paintings present similar problems for historians: one group appreciated that neither a photographer nor an artist is neutral in recording the past.

Combining Thinking Skills with photographs as sources certainly increased motivation and enjoyment for both the students and myself. The lesson was more animated and lively than previous skills-based lessons. Students were left with a sense of achievement, and felt more confident about the value of their own ideas. The students were asked one final question: *'What do you think history is all about?'* One student replied *'interpretation'*. I was most relieved, given that this had been an underlying theme for a whole term's work! I concluded by pointing out that 'interpretation' is about presenting ideas which are credible, based on historical evidence. Training in *thinking* is therefore a fundamental building block for the study of history. One student who had said little all lesson, and who is recognised as being the most quiet and shy student in the group, remarked *'That's all that separates me from a professional historian then – training in how to think!'*

Resource 2

Sources of Photographs

1   Clive Hardy & Paul Harris *Tyneside at War* Archive Publications, 1988.

2   Juliet Gardner *The People's War*, Collins and Brown, 1991.

3   Juliet Gardner *The People's War*, Collins and Brown, 1991.

4   Nigel Kelly & Martyn Whittock *The Era of the Second World War* Heinemann, 1993.

5   R J Cootes & L E Snellgrove *The Era of the Second World War* Nelson, 1994.

6   Juliet Gardner *The People's War* Collins and Brown, 1991.

7   Clive Hardy & Paul Harris *Tyneside at War* Archive Publications, 1988.

8   Juliet Gardner *The People's War* Collins and Brown, 1991.

9   Clive Hardy & Paul Harris *Tyneside at War* Archive Publications, 1988.

10 Clive Hardy & Paul Harris *Tyneside at War* Archive Publications, 1988.

11 Clive Hardy & Paul Harris *Tyneside at War* Archive Publications, 1988.

12 Juliet Gardner *The People's War* Collins and Brown, 1991.

13 Juliet Gardner *The People's War* Collins and Brown, 1991.

14 R J Cootes & L E Snellgrove *The Era of the Second World War* Nelson, 1994.

Task Sheet

Task 1

a) Record your results on *Recording Grid 1*. Sort your photographs into themes. When you are happy with your themes, record them in *Column B*, and record the relevant numbers in *Column A*.

b) Draw a curly bracket around two themes and say how they link together.

c) Briefly discuss how you decided on your themes. Explain your method in *Recording Grid 1, Column D*.

d) Can you think of any other themes? Record any that you come up with in *Recording Grid 2*. Did you use a different method to create these themes? If so record them in *Column D*.

Task 2

Photograph 3 has the following caption:

> *The Home Guard kept a lookout for suspicious persons, including survivors from shot down enemy planes. In this training exercise, a man dressed as a woman pretends to shoot a guard at a roadblock.*

a) In your groups, produce an alternative caption for Photograph 3.

b) Discuss the problems historians face when using photographic sources.

c) Choose one other picture, which could easily be misleading. As a group, write your own caption for the photograph. Be prepared to explain and justify your choice in a class discussion.

Task 3

a) Choose 2 photographs and discuss the witting and unwitting evidence which they contain. Record your findings on the Grid.

b) How would knowledge of the period and the photographer change your findings? Which column would this knowledge affect most? What does this tell you about using photographs?

Task 4

Choose 1 photograph each, which you think the Government would have been eager to publish. Write down your reasons. Be prepared to present your ideas to the rest of the class later. Also note down how you decided, and what questions you asked yourself in order to make your choice.

Task 1: Recording Grid 1

A Photograph number:	B Theme:	C Link (with explanation):	D Methodology:

Task 1: Recording Grid 2

A	B	C	D
Photograph number:	Theme:	Link (with explanation):	Methodology:

Task 2:

a) Alternative caption for photograph 3:

b) Problems using photographs:

c) Alternative caption for another photograph:

Photo Number:

Caption:

Task 3:		
Photo Number:	**Witting**	**Unwitting**

Task 4:

Photo:

Reasons for publication:

Task 4:

Photo:

Thinking Through History

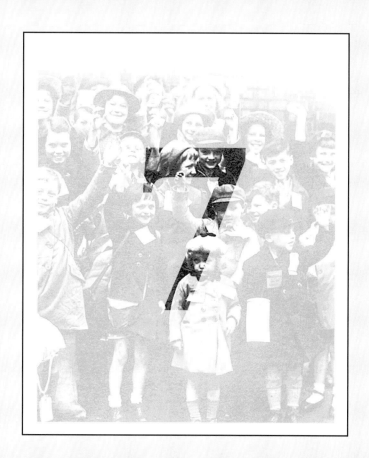

Pictures from Memory

7 Pictures from Memory

Rationale

To develop understanding one needs to think about the object of study or to process it. Pupils are asked to think about information presented in the form of written or spoken language. We generally ask pupils to learn or revise from text. We don't give much attention to decoding visual imagery. The point has been made elsewhere (see p68) in relation to **Reading Photographs and Pictures**.

Pictures from Memory was originally conceived as a 'different' lesson in geography that would begin to make pupils think harder about how they see, make sense of and remember visual information – maps, sketches, photographs and diagrams. The technique also holds good for history.

Pupils are asked to look at an image for ten seconds, without the aid of paper and pen and then recreate the image. This is done as a group task, with each individual taking a turn to 'look' and then add to the collective drawing. Not only is there a great deal of individual processing to do – but just think about the group processes that go on. This task cannot be done successfully unless the group works together. As a result this Strategy is a prime candidate for beginning to unpack issues about working together to learn. Learning is not just an individual activity.

In common with other Thinking Skills Strategies, attempting the task becomes much more than a simple 'draw' or 'copy' individual activity. It involves the application of **Key Skills**. The pupils are exposed to learning situations whereby they have to *work with others*, to *problem solve*, and to *communicate* their *team based findings*. In addition, by evaluating each group's strategies pupils may come to learn valuable lessons in *improving their own learning and performance*.

The great majority of pupils think this activity is great, but, as usual, the challenge for the teacher is to distil the learning potential from the task. You will find that you are battling against the deeply entrenched utilitarian notion that many pupils have that 'only writing in books equals work'. The challenge in using the Strategy is to open your pupils' eyes to the art of seeing and remembering. If you need to justify this Strategy to yourself (or others) consider how much visual information is provided to pupils in GCSE exams. Most low-achieving pupils do not make good use of such information. If pupils are asked to learn from pictures, maps or diagrams, do they have strategies to do this, or even a language to talk about the analysis of visual sources?

Medieval Life

Context

This activity was used as part of our approach to the 'medieval realms' Area of Study in Year 7. We have used the approach successfully with pupils of all abilities in our all-boys year group, including those with SEN. The lesson was one of a series within our scheme of work on 'medieval life' and was used as a visual introduction for the pupils' investigation into life of a medieval peasant.

The intended learning outcomes were:

- to increase knowledge and understanding of characteristic features of the medieval period (2a);
- to encourage the pupils to discover a range of models for remembering information;
- to utilise pupils' visual memory as another tool in the learning process;
- to develop pupils' abilities to identify, select and use pictures as a basis for historical enquiries (4a);
- and last, but not least, to introduce the topic in a stimulating and more attractive way.

The follow-up exercise was a form of self assessment for the pupils to investigate how successful their respective learning strategies had been, by evaluating how they had assimilated the visual source used.

> A useful rehearsal of a **key skill**: *improving and evaluating one's own learning.*

Preparation

The picture – a black and white artist's impression – was taken from *Contrasts and Connections* in John Murray's SHP Series, which we enlarged to A4 size (for the SEN pupils and those with visual impairment, the picture can be enlarged to A3 size). (see *Resource 1*)

> This technique is easily transferable to any appropriate, linked, visual source.

We prepared the classroom by putting the desks into groups of four before the lesson began (five groups in all). There was no account taken of friendship or ability groupings, we chose the pupils at random. On either side of the teacher's desk, two copies of the picture were stuck down with BluTack.

Launching

As an introduction to the activity we asked the pupils to visualise a room in their house, in which they spent a good deal of their waking hours. We asked a couple of pupils for a very brief description of the room they were thinking about. This exercise took no more than five minutes.

Instructions

1 Each pupil in a group was given a number from 1 to 4. Each group was then given a single sheet of plain A4 paper, a pencil and a rubber.

2 It was explained to the pupils that on the teacher's desk was a picture of a house, and that by the end of the lesson they were going to have reproduced this picture from memory on the blank piece of A4 paper.

Three particular points were stressed. Firstly, each group should decide for themselves what and how they should record what they needed. Secondly, the group should organise what each 'runner' should observe and record, round by round. Thirdly, that to stand a good chance of success, all individuals within the group would need to co-operate in order to complete the task.

3 All pupils Numbered 1 were instructed to come out to the teacher's desk and look at the picture for 20 seconds, with no paper, pencil or pen to hand. Whilst they were doing this, the others were told to talk quietly amongst themselves.

4 After 20 seconds the Number 1 pupils returned to their groups and were told to transfer what they had seen onto the A4 piece of paper. No other instructions were given here, allowing the pupils to communicate their knowledge in their own way.

This stage could be reduced to one more 'final' visit per group.

5 After 1 minute, Number 2 pupils were told to come up to the teacher's desk, and the above process was repeated, both for them and then for pupils numbered 3 and 4, in turn.

6 The whole exercise was repeated, with each pupil going up twice, and adding to the picture.

As this was happening the teacher went round the classroom observing interactions within the groups, but giving no further guidance as to how to successfully complete the task.

Managing the activity

It is important to keep a very close check on the timing of each pupil's visit to the main picture and their 'drawing time' within their groups in order to ensure the lesson maintains a brisk pace and encourage the pupils to remain on task. Obviously, the very nature of the task requires pupils to move around the classroom. So, be prepared! We found that the activity should take no longer than 15 minutes in all.

It is also vital that the pupils are made aware that it is their *memory* skills being tested and not their *artistic* abilities. Therefore any verbal communications between the pupil at the front and his/her group is to be discouraged.

A worthwhile point of focus, alternatively an OHT or an interactive whiteboard could be used.

Debriefing

This was used to encourage the pupils to improve their cognitive skills and to help make them aware of how they remember pictorial information. This can be achieved in several different ways.

In this instance, as a visible point of reference, we stuck an enlarged A3 copy of the original picture at the front of the classroom. We then asked each group to nominate a spokesperson to come out and stick his group's version next to it and explain to the class how they had gone about reproducing the picture.

There were varying responses from the groups:

The 'pros' and 'cons' of a group adopting various strategies – even in advance of seeing the picture – are fruitful areas to quiz the pupils upon.

- dividing the pictures into quarters, with each pupil within a group being responsible for reproducing one segment of the picture;
- reproducing the picture from the top to the bottom (or vice versa);
- Number 1 pupil looking at the whole picture, while Numbers 2 to 4 looked at specific parts of it;
- one group mentioned that they concentrated on the centre of the picture first, with the parts around the outside being left to last;
- one group of pupils seemed to remember the most obvious parts of the picture first, eg the shape of the roof, animals and the treasure chest.

We then asked the pupils to consider which would appear to them to be the most effective approach, ie which picture had the most accurate and useful information in it. Would they change the way that they had completed the task in a future lesson?

Important links emerge here with regard to the learning power of iconic learning.

An important part of such a Thinking Skills lesson is to encourage the pupils to think about how they would use their skills and transfer them to other situations. In the debriefing section of this lesson, which took up some 10 minutes, the pupils highlighted the obvious links with revision strategies and the effectiveness of learning through pictorial rather than written evidence.

An example of 'near transfer' (see page 138).

We also discussed the impact of 'seeing' images of places where the pupils had been – on school visits, or family holidays – as being more easily 'remembered' than in trying to recall information which they had read about, watched or had been told about.

Follow-up

The follow-up was a homework task where individual pupils were instructed to draw a version of the picture in their exercise books, labelling at least five features which they could remember, for example the animals inside the hut, or the meat hanging from the ceiling.

Inside a peasant's dwelling

From *Contrasts and Connections*,
John Murray

Exemplar 2

Motte and Bailey Castle

Context

This Strategy has been trialled with several mixed ability Year 7 groups as well as 'banded' ability groups in Year 9. In one Year 7 lesson a drawing of a motte and bailey castle was used from within the Study Area of the Study Unit 'Britain 1066-1500'. It followed work on William's problems, and solutions in ruling England after 1066. The learning outcomes linked to the National Curriculum were:

- to develop the pupils' range and depth of historical knowledge and understanding;
- to assist the pupils to organise and communicate historical information more effectively.

By undertaking the task I hoped that the pupils would learn to realise the utility of the whole picture and the details within it. Finally, I hoped to offer the pupils an insight into their own most effective learning styles.

Preparation

It may be useful, but not always necessary, to select the groups beforehand to enable a combination of high ability and lower ability within the group. I found that it worked best with random group selection, especially in Year 7, since they were still relatively new to each other and might benefit from, even enjoy, working outside their own friendship groups. The pupils will need to work quite closely together and therefore it is useful to seat all four around one table. Try to ensure a clear space at the front of the classroom because almost a quarter of the class will need to stand together to look at the picture for their given time. Or you could request pupils to view two identical pictures. Also try to ensure clear gangways and access as the children inevitably dash back to their groups at great speed to ensure that they retain all the information!

Launching

The element of surprise is useful in this exercise and so there is very little in the way of a content introduction for this Exemplar. If this is your first attempt at a Thinking Skills lesson then it may be as well to admit this to the class, for example: *'We are going to do something a little bit different today. It doesn't involve too much writing – in fact it is more drawing!'* Ask the pupils how information is presented in books – the intended answer is of course: writing *and* pictures. *'Do we use pictures enough?'* *'Hands up how many of you have come across a picture today since you got up this morning?'* *'Can you remember it?'* *'Can you explain why or why not?'* This will hopefully introduce the idea to the pupils that pictures are all around us, as part of our everyday lives, so they are not something we should dismiss out of hand. I am especially referring to those pupils who may see drawing pictures in a history lesson as pointless, and consequently a low-level task. This may be because what really concerns them is: *'I can't draw, Miss'*.

Instructions

It is important that instructions are particularly clear in this activity. The pupils must be aware that they have only a limited amount of time when they view the original (I suggest no more than 30 seconds per viewing), and that only **one** large copy is to be reproduced by each group. It is important that they work together as a group to help each other, and that everyone contributes to the actual drawing of the picture. Once you have given the instructions, allow the pupils a couple of minutes to discuss how they are going to attempt this activity. After several trials, I found it useful to allow each child to view the picture twice especially if this is their first attempt at the activity. There are a variety of reasons for this: it allows the children to rethink their strategy as a group and as an individual; it enables them to communicate effectively about what they saw and what they need to look for; and generally the children are keen and enthusiastic to 'have another go'.

Managing the activity

One of the learning outcomes of this activity is to improve pupils' ability to recall information. With this in mind it is useful for the teacher to keep a close eye on the master copy of the picture to avoid any cheating! It is also beneficial for the teacher to circulate the classroom observing the pupils working in groups and to make appropriate comments on the negative and positive aspects of group work that are on view. It is also helpful, and sometimes necessary, for the teacher to write down some informal notes about what actually happened in each group, and to note pupils' conversation about the task. This will help to keep the teacher occupied so that they are not as tempted to interrupt the pupils at work. This 'listening period' can be used to the teacher's advantage in debriefing the activity.

Debriefing

There are a variety of important issues that can be tackled in debriefing this lesson. It can be interesting and productive to compare and contrast the pupils' work by temporarily displaying each drawing with the original. By doing this it is clearly visible to the pupils what is common to all the drawings, and furthermore what is different. Issues of competitiveness may be diffused by more pointed, open questions relating to degrees of co-operation achieved. This enables the class to decide which one is the nearest replica and to justify their choice. It may be that there is one feature that many, if not all the groups have missed out. For example, in one class I taught no one had included any labels in their drawing and many groups had missed out the title of the drawing.

The early phase of debriefing could be content-led as you ask the pupils about *what* they have learned about the castle, for example:

'What are the two main parts of the castle?'

'What is it made of?'

'Where is it located?'

'What are the strengths and weakness of this type of castle?'

This will generate a good discussion and demonstrate how much the pupils have learned about motte and bailey castles – possibly without realising it themselves. It is useful to point this out to them in terms of a summary of what they have learned simply from a drawing.

This can feed directly into the more complex debriefing questions, for example:

'How did you do it?'

'What strategies did you use?'

'What skills have you used in this lesson?'

'Could you transfer what you have learned in this lesson to another context?'

The answers to these questions will vary greatly. But be prepared for puzzled looks as the pupils initially reply *'We just did it'*. It is from this basic standpoint that you need to elicit from the pupils a more detailed and thoughtful answer. If the class is really finding it difficult to answer, it is helpful to use the notes you made during the activity in order to prompt and coax answers from them. Amongst the types of strategies pupils use are:

- the first person gets the outline of the picture and the rest fill in the details;
- some groups divide the picture into four sections and each pupil is assigned a quarter of the picture to focus on;
- some groups do not have a formal strategy but ask pupils to look at specific areas when they look at the picture, for example *'You look at what is to the right of the castle'*.

Some important themes can be brought out from asking *'How did you do it?'* If you are concerned with how well they worked as a group, ask *'Did you communicate effectively?'* *'Did you help each other?'* *'Did you ask questions of each other to decide if what you remembered was correct?'* This activity challenges their ability to work as a group and communicate effectively. It can also be appropriate when debriefing to ask the pupils if they would make any changes or alterations to their strategy if they did this activity again, or whether they would use a more formal strategy next time.

Finally in debriefing ask the pupils if they can transfer the skills and knowledge they have learned in this lesson to another school subject, context or within history itself. In answering this, the pupils sometimes recognise that although you often need the whole picture of an event, it is also the details that matter. Pupils usually agree that they are more likely to remember this picture because they have been forced to think about it and discuss it rather than copy it. This has implications for revision. They also say that their memory has been tested during the activity, which again links in to revision. When asked for connections with other subjects they mention art, where they have to look at the whole picture as well as the detail, and also any subject where they have to remember diagrams, for example the water cycle in science.

Follow-up

The lesson was used as an introduction to medieval castles. In the follow-up the children found out about other types of castles, and then wrote up a medieval guide for someone visiting a castle. The guide had to include: what the castle looks like, what it was made from and what its strengths and weaknesses were. In the follow-up lesson it is interesting to ask the pupils how much they have remembered from the previous lesson. For the many times I have trialled it, I've always been impressed by how much they do remember.

A motte and bailey castle

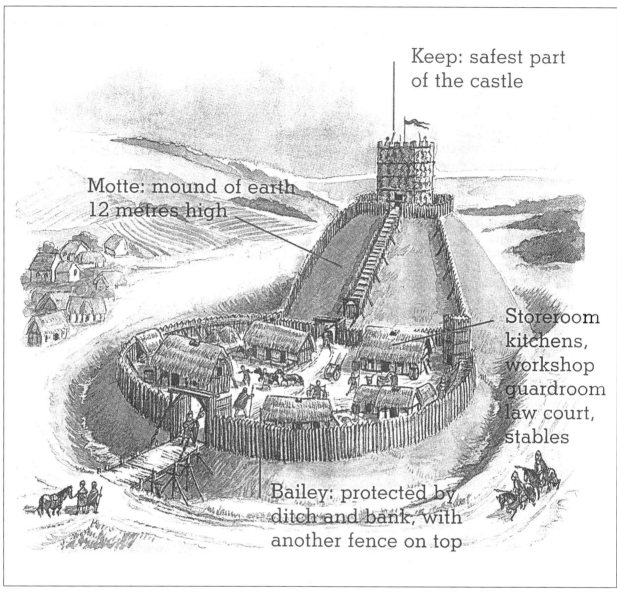

Keep: safest part of the castle

Motte: mound of earth 12 metres high

Storeroom kitchens, workshop guardroom law court, stables

Bailey: protected by ditch and bank, with another fence on top

From *Quest: The Medieval World*, (1998), Stanley Thornes Limited

Thinking Through History

Story-telling

8 Story-telling

Rationale

Stories are powerful media. They are one of the main ways in which societies transmit their culture from generation to generation. One of the few images we have of children being riveted at school is the infant class sitting on the floor while their teacher reads a story. Somehow teaching in secondary schools, perhaps with the exception of English, has lost its grip on story-telling.

The inclusion of story-telling as a central method to teach and learn history has ebbed and flowed along with changing educational agendas. The 'narrative tradition' particularly held sway at times when learning history was regarded as a worthy vehicle to transmit moral virtues to pupils, through the stories relating to the biographies of 'significant' people reacting to past events, and simultaneously, by inculcating a strong sense of national identity and patriotism amongst their audience.

> Stories can provide an ideal access point for pupils to break through the essential abstractions in studying history, ie the distances and differences in time, place, actions, and attitudes.

Story-telling in secondary history went out of fashion through its erroneous connotations with pupil 'passivity' and the growth of 'skills-based' approaches. However, in recent years the benefits of skilled story-telling have been re-appraised. Teaching through stories can act as a superb vehicle to return people back into the past. As Egan (1995) claims, they can *fire* the child's imagination. The story's narrative can act as a ready made springboard to create bite-sized chunks of problematic thinking, relating characters to problems, dilemmas and issues.

Other advantages can be summarised as follows:

> Story-telling helps appeal to all the senses.

- stories put history into real life contexts with real people (or occasionally, made-up ones) providing topicality and relevance;
- stories provide a context and focus for developing listening skills, often sadly lacking in many students;
- stories are a vehicle for teaching students how to remember, which receives little explicit attention in the curriculum;
- storyboarding helps to develop sequencing skills which are an essential 'mental superstructure' to help students explain and present their ideas;

> Story-telling can operate at different cognitive and conceptual levels: both the micro – through providing sufficient context and scaffolding – to reveal the macro level.

- using stories exposes students to extended pieces of text, rarely encountered elsewhere in history, which therefore helps prepare them for examination papers;
- finally, story-telling can be the key to unlocking understanding some of history's 'big concepts', such as causation, change and effect.

This is a strong pedigree. Moreover, stories do not lose their fascination. Amongst adults the popularity of the historical narrative – as feature films, TV drama or novels – is testimony to their enduring interest.

Telling stories in history is not frivolous, nor a distraction, or 'low-level' classroom activity. Their capacity to motivate appears to be almost universal. Just think about how pupils react to your introductory remark: *'I'm going to tell you a story'*. Stories are also an excellent means to develop thinking, especially when done with thought and care, as the following Exemplars suggest. Try them and see.

Adapting the Strategy

These Exemplars are easily adapted to other story-telling techniques. For example *The Hundred Days* can be – and has been – used as a 1, 2, 3 exercise (see *Exemplar 1*). Likewise, with some minor reduction in content, The Spanish Armada could be used with either of the other two techniques. Furthermore, history lends itself perfectly to almost any event, or story, being adapted by individual teachers and taught in any one of these ways.

The Spanish Armada

Context

This Strategy was used in Year 8 for the Area of Study 'Britain 1500-1750'. I have tried it, successfully, with pupils in Year 8 of all abilities within our fully comprehensive cohort. The lesson was one of a series of lessons on Elizabethan England, so the pupils had some prior knowledge of the period, although the topic of the Spanish Armada was new to most of them. Most of the detail here relates to a top-band Year 8 group. They are a pleasant class, well motivated and enthusiastic, though I have found this same Strategy has worked equally well with less able pupils. In fact, it has helped to motivate some of the less enthusiastic pupils.

Although the Spanish Armada was the context for the Strategy, I was more concerned with the processes the pupils went through. I have since used the same activity in different contexts with several groups in all Years from 7 to 12.

As well as the outcome of developing knowledge and understanding of a key event in Tudor England (2a,c) the intended learning outcomes were:

- to provide pupils with a number of alternative models for remembering information;
- to make the pupils aware that they can learn and remember in many different ways;
- to stimulate different ways of enhancing knowledge and understanding;
- to encourage the pupils to tap into their visual memory as a way of learning;
- to explore the possibilities of processing and recording information in alternative ways, according to pupils' preferred learning styles.

> This mix of outcomes represents worthwhile synthesis of historical knowledge, skills and understanding together with insights into metacognitive learning strategies.

The follow-up exercise also aims to improve their organisation and communication skills (5a,c) through the practice of selection, and sequencing information.

Preparation

My story of the Armada was adapted from a number of textbook versions of the story. By 'customising' it I was able to make it more suitable to the activity. I also found that this 'sense of ownership' helped me to get to know the story well, so I was able later to create emphases and voice modulations or intonations wherever necessary.

> A necessary and important step for maximum 'performance value'.

I decided to work with groups of 3, so before the lesson I thought of likely trios, taking ability and friendship into account. This helped in the smooth transition from the *launching* task into the activity itself. The Strategy involves having to leave two-thirds of the class unattended briefly, or at least otherwise engaged in the same room for a short period of time. As a colleague was not available to help, I decided to return the last piece of homework I had marked and encouraged the other pupils to discuss it in pairs.

Launching

I have tried a number of different ways in to this activity and the most successful ones have involved linking to the pupils' previous knowledge of stories, songs or fairy tales. Typically, I would ask them if anyone can name me a famous story, real or fictional. This tends to provoke responses such as Red Riding Hood or other fairy tales, myths or fables. I then choose one of these and ask them to tell the story and see who knows it. Invariably, this can be used to show that we often remember a story better than separate facts because the events of a story are linked together, in a chain of events. I have also used the words to nursery rhymes as an example, and quizzed the pupils as to why everyone seems to know all the words in the correct order. You can then link by explaining that many events in history are nothing but stories: they should therefore be easier to remember!

After this introduction, I read out the groups and numbered group members 1, 2, and 3. If you do not have a total number of pupils divisible by three, I would suggest making the last group or two into groups of four and having two pupils as number 3 in those groups. I had handed out the last homework to the pupils so I asked the 2s and the 3s to discuss this in pairs, while I gathered all the 1s together at the front of the room. You could consider using colleagues or PGCE students if available, to keep an eye on your 2s and 3s if you want to take your 1s to another classroom.

> Such classroom management practicalities demand careful planning.

Instructions

1 I gathered the number 1s together and told them I was going to read them a story which they had to try and remember, because they had to re-tell it to the number 2s, who would then have to re-tell it to the number 3s. They were not allowed to take any written notes.

2 I read the story through once, at a leisurely pace, and at the end asked if there were any questions. After answering any questions and checking they knew what to do I sent them back to their groups.

3 At this stage, I had to isolate the number 3s, so gathered them together at the front of the room. The number 1s then retold the story to the number 2s. Again the 2s were allowed to ask any questions of the 1s and were encouraged to go over the story themselves.

4 The number 3s were then allowed back to their groups, where I instructed the 2s to tell them the story. I told the 1s to just listen at first and then, if there was anything they thought the 2s had missed out, they could add in extra details at the end.

5 As this was happening, I went round each group and asked for any volunteers amongst the number 3s who would be willing to re-tell the story to the whole class. There were five who were happy to do this and I felt it would be better to ask each one to feedback separately, so I asked them to wait outside the room, trusting them not to discuss the story, as I asked each one to come back in individually and re-tell the story.

> Important cognitive skills come into play in the telling and re-telling phases.

Managing the activity

This is possibly one of the riskier Strategies, but certainly one of the most powerful and worthwhile. It is important to maintain a decent pace throughout the activity and to keep a check on the timing. I would also advise maintaining a sense of purpose throughout the activity: the pupils should enjoy it but they should be encouraged to realise that they are learning as well.

> The basis of this problem-solving task is co-operation.

> An indicator of success and motivation!

When the 1s are telling the story to the 2s, and likewise when the 2s retell it to the 3s, I would suggest circulating round each group, listening very carefully. It is also very useful to take brief notes of what they are saying: these can be of invaluable use in the debriefing. I would also advise not to get involved in any of the discussions: the pupils should be encouraged to rely on their own skills.

> Keep in mind throughout that the teacher's role is one of a manager and **facilitator** of learning.

Debriefing

This activity encourages the pupils to use many cognitive skills. In order to develop these, debriefing is an important opportunity. I would strongly suggest leaving at least 20 minutes to debrief a 50-60 minute lesson as this is the key to enhancing their metacognitive skills. It should be used to make them realise there are different ways of learning and remembering. They should be encouraged to realise that **learning how to remember** is an invaluable skill and certainly worth persevering with.

> Evidence of developing **metacognition**.

I started with the question *'What things did you remember?'* The discussion focused on the most common things that most number 3s had remembered. I encouraged the number 1s to chip in with any extra details they remembered that the number 3s did not. I also encouraged pupils to correct each other if any details were inaccurate (care must be taken here to do this positively!). The most commonly recalled details tended to be names, dates, figures and amusing sections (like the mouldy biscuits). I made sure I praised them at this stage: between them they had remembered virtually all of the story.

> This range of responses reveals interesting insights into how pupils (and adults?) remember and recall historical episodes and events.

The next question I asked was *'How did you remember what you remembered?'* I think this is the most important one, so I try to spend a long time on this. Don't be put off if you don't get an immediate response – you normally don't! Wait for a while, let the question sink in, allow the pupils 'thinking time' and don't be tempted to put words into their mouths! The most important way of remembering (apart from 'it just stuck') to come out of my debriefing seemed to be:

- trying to focus on the important things, like names and dates, and things like the crescent shape;
- remembering the interesting things, like the fireships or the beacons;

- remembering any details that were different or funny;
- saying it over and over to yourself;
- picturing some of the scenes and seeing the story as a movie in your mind;
- thinking of things that rhyme with key words;
- thinking of people you know, to remind you of people in the story; (one child thought of her uncle Philip)
- seeing it as a chain of events in your mind; (when I quizzed the pupil who said this I asked him what came after a certain event in the story and he remembered exactly)
- remembering it as a map in your head.

To prompt them slightly here you can ask them '*What helped you remember certain things?*' Most of them agreed they learnt more this way so I asked them '*Why?*' and typical responses were '*saying it to others helps it stick in your head*', '*when you've got to pass it on to someone, you make yourself remember it more*' and '*the pressure of having to remember it to tell it on*'. I think it's important to ask them to summarise what skills they have learnt or used during this activity and I also asked them '*Could you use these skills elsewhere?*' An important element of thinking skills lessons and debriefing them is to encourage the pupils to think about using their skills in other situations. Encouraging answers to this question included '*You could use it to help you revise*' and '*You could use it with friends when trying to remember things for the next lesson or a test*'.

We agreed at the end that there are many different ways of remembering things, that remembering is certainly a skill that can be learnt and improved upon, and that we can apply it to other situations as well as revising for tests.

Follow-up

This is an important feature of this Strategy. It can be used as a means of encouraging pupils to think about causation, chronology and selection of information. The follow-up activity should take about an hour, adding to the first hour on the story-telling and debriefing. It could be worth re-capping on their debriefing responses at the start of the lesson.

The follow-up involves a storyboarding exercise. The students were given a storyboard sheet with 8 frames and were asked to re-tell the story using just these eight frames. You can use the resource as it is or get them to cut and paste the frames into their exercise books. Further, they were only allowed to use 8 words in each frame as this encourages them to be selective in their choice of words as well as in the importance of events. I have been surprised that many pupils find this sequencing and selecting quite difficult. Common problems were using too many frames up early on, or not using enough and having some left over. It is worthwhile encouraging the pupils to do it in pencil first. They also seem to have difficulty in summarising each frame into eight words. An alternative way of doing this activity (which some of my colleagues prefer) is to allow the pupils to draw the scene as well as writing eight words, as this helps some pupils tap into their visual memory.

You can further debrief this storyboarding activity by focusing on what events they included and how they decided upon them. You could also choose some of the pupils to read theirs out and encourage comment on how it could be improved. This needs care. Although we should be encouraging pupils to criticise each other constructively, it must not become demoralising. As a further task, perhaps with more able groups, a longer piece of work of more extended writing could be set.

Storyboarding is certainly an appropriate follow-up, since it involves crucial historical skills: visualisation; solution; sequencing; summarising; and establishing significance.

Resource 1

Story: The Spanish Armada

King Philip of Spain was a Roman Catholic. He had once been married to Mary I. Long after her death, he still wanted to make England a Catholic country. He decided to attack England. He set about creating a great fleet of ships called the Spanish Armada and in July 1588 the Armada set sail for England. It was July 19th when the English spotted it. Beacons were lit on the hilltops to carry the news across the country. Meanwhile, down in Plymouth, the English Commander, Lord Howard, made his plans with Sir Francis Drake.

There were 130 Spanish ships, painted in red and gold, covering 11km of sea. The Spanish formed themselves into a crescent shape, making it very difficult for the English to attack. So, day and night for a week, there was a running fight, as the English chased the Armada up the English Channel.

On July 27th, the Armada dropped anchor near the port of Calais, ready to pick up troops in the Netherlands. This gave the English their chance. Eight ships, carrying tar and with their guns loaded, were set on fire and set towards the Spanish vessels. As soon as they saw these floating bombs, the Spanish panicked. They raised their anchors and sailed off into the night.

Only one Spanish galleon went aground. But, by morning, something far more important had happened. The Armada had been scattered. The crescent shape had been broken at last.

When the English closed in to attack, the Spanish ships still fought back bravely. Most of them survived but they were badly battered. They had only one hope – to head for home. They could not go through the Channel because they would have been easy targets for the English. Instead, they tried to sail north, round Scotland.

Nearly every ship was damaged. Masts were broken and sails torn. On board, sick and wounded men had to drink stale water and eat mouldy biscuits. One ship was tied up with cables so that it did not fall apart! Many of these ships and men never did reach home. Some galleons were wrecked off Scotland; others were destroyed off the Irish coast. Their sailors staggered ashore, only to be killed by the Irish.

Only 67 ships got back to Spain. Few of them were fit to put to sea again. It was a sad end for such a great fleet.

The Atomic Bomb

Context

This activity was used with three Year 9 classes covering the full range of ability from a 'top set' to an SEN set. On each occasion the material was modified to suit the audience. In particular the debriefing session was shortened for the lower abilities. The lesson was used as an introduction to the dropping of the atom bombs upon Hiroshima and Nagasaki in 1945 as part of the Study Unit 'The Twentieth Century World'. The follow-up lesson took the form of a debate on the moral and ethical aspects: whether the Americans should have dropped these weapons without warning upon civilian cities. We explored the many issues and controversies involved in the topic. The fact that pupils had a good understanding of the devastation caused by the bombs from the story-telling lesson kept them focused on the essential issues during the debate and reinforced the seriousness of what they were discussing.

> The impact of the story-telling Strategy possibly contributed to the success of this follow-up lesson.

The story engaged the interest of all three classes easily, and the length of it did not seem to be a problem for the lower-ability pupils, as one of the skills being developed is their ability to select the important information.

The intended learning outcomes were:

- to enhance pupil knowledge and understanding (2a);
- to encourage pupils to sequence key events (1);
- to improve their ability to select key points of an event and judge their significance (2a,b,c,e);
- to personalise a controversial and somewhat alien issue (2a,b);
- to improve pupils' ability to recall information by encouraging them to explore different methods of recording and remembering an event (4a,b,5a,b,c);
- to tap into pupils' visual memory skills (4a,b,5a,b,c,d).

Preparation

The story was made up by myself using information from various sources and newspaper articles from the time. Words that would be difficult to record by the pupils, eg Hiroshima and Nagasaki were deliberately left out, along with some of the more gory details of the destruction caused. The story was deliberately told from an individual's point of view in order to personalise their experience, and so aid pupils' understanding. However, it also includes a lot of factual detail, because that is what I wanted them to be able to recall. Prior to the lesson it helps to rehearse the story a few times so you are familiar with its presentation in order that it flows more easily.

The class needs to be divided into the four 'method' groupings according to what they will be asked to do with the information, ie a group of 'examiners', a group of 'listeners', a group of 'writers', and a group of 'drawers'. Later on the 'examiners' will need to pair up with the 'writers' to test their accuracy, so I found it worked best to have the rooms set out in rows of pairs and gave each row a different method to use. One 'examiner' from each pair can then swap seats with a 'writer' when it comes to being tested.

> This Strategy offers pupils access into the three very different learning styles.

Launching

I wanted to focus pupils on the purpose of the activity from the start, so I asked them: 'Tell me, if you have just seen a burglary would you remember what happened better than if you just read about it in a newspaper. Why?' We concluded that if you see something you remember it better. A link was then made to the activity by saying that we were going to do an experiment to test whether we thought that was true. The class was divided up according to the method they would be using and the 'writers' and 'drawers' were given either lined or plain paper.

> Similar issues here as in Exemplar 1 (page 101).

Instructions

Of the four groups one will be 'examiners' and should be given a checklist so they know the stories being retold are accurate (see Resource 3), the second will be 'listeners', the third 'writers' who record the story in words, and the fourth are only allowed to 'draw' (although numbers and symbols are allowed).

> Teaching Thinking Through History Strategies sometimes demand a high level of classroom craft and management skills.

All four groups listen to the story which should be read at a normal – or possibly slightly slower speed – with plenty of appropriate expression. Once the story is finished, allow a

Such Strategies place a premium on Vygotskyan principles, namely the development of subject-related talk and structured, paired talk through co-operation.

couple of minutes for the 'writers' and 'drawers' to fill in any blanks or add details. Each person from the 'listening' groups should then be allocated to an 'examiner,' to whom they retell the story, trying to remember as much detail as possible. They will be given one mark for every main point they recall, another if they remember it in the right order and an extra point for any extra details. These are ticked off on the checklist by the 'examiner'. Meanwhile the 'writers' and 'drawers' can be looking at their accounts and trying to memorise them. There should be **no communication** between the groups, as this will affect the experiment. Once the 'listeners' group has been 'examined' the 'examiners' can check the 'writers' whilst the 'listeners' can examine the 'drawers' versions.

Managing the activity

Although the activity does involve some moving around I was pleased that most groups behaved well. The fact that the pupils got to 'examine' each other within a set framework seemed to be a novel experience which especially motivated them.

Debriefing

The debrief is essential to this activity, therefore at least twenty minutes out of a fifty-minute lesson should be allocated for a proper discussion. Try to base the questions on the aims of the lesson which are to find out what their preferred learning style is, to encourage them to think about what makes good listening, and to help them remember and recall information better. The questioning should therefore focus on the *process* by which each group remembered and recalled the information **(metacognition)**, ie *'How did you try to remember the information?'* Comparisons should also be made between the different approaches which had been taken and what the advantages and disadvantages were of each method. A helpful device is to draw up a 'pros and cons checklist' through Q/A on the board (or OHT). Also would they use the same method again, were they to repeat the activity? And why or why not? To encourage **bridging** and **transference** of the skills used it would be useful to ask in what other situations they could use these skills, and for which other subjects it might be useful.

The first time I used this Strategy I expected a lively discussion to ensue, where pupils would give lengthy, extended answers – and was disappointed. Instead I almost had to drag the answers out of them! On reflection I realised that the question I wanted them to answer, ie *'What helps you remember information better?'* was actually too demanding and required a great deal of thought. Consequently, I have learnt to allow the pupils time to think before answering and have taught myself to hold back rather than plunging into the inevitable silence and putting the answers into their mouths. Talking about their thinking processes is something pupils need time to get used to and that comes with practice: the more they do it, the more they will feel comfortable talking about how they did it. Also, I tried to intervene as little as possible with my own ideas. When a pupil gives a short answer, eg *'I saw pictures in my head'*, I will simply ask them to explain their thinking further, rather than reiterating what they've said (which is very tempting to do!).

In my view, by the end of the lesson, each of the main outcomes had been met.

One useful way of helping pupils to analyse what they did is to ask them to fill in a student learning log (see *Resource 4*). This allows them more time to reflect and usually generates a more in-depth discussion. Naturally some pupils may feel under pressure to write what you want to hear, but it does help them focus on the important aspects within the task – like **transfer** and the role of the teacher. Within the Department we have found that a concentration upon such processes has yielded valuable insights into pupils' levels of understanding as well as our own professional craft practices. We have developed our own skills in debriefing techniques.

Follow-up

Pupils could be asked to select what they see as the six most important points and draw them as a storyboard. This will develop their ability to select, and also helps them to visualise the events. Alternatively they could be asked to describe the events which they think would have led up to the events which took place in the story, or continue the story afterwards. This will encourage them to consider the causes or consequences of the atom bombs. Another suggestion is that they could re-write the story from the point of view of someone else: the pilot who dropped the bomb, an American journalist, or the Japanese Emperor.

The idea of peer-review or assessment with agreed criteria is a popular technique within the Department, and is undertaken within many history classrooms.

Here the teacher has re-focused the lesson back to its original principles.

Fine notion of a Student Learning Log extends the opportunities for student self-assessment/evaluation and metacognition.

Story: The Atomic Bomb

I was twelve years old when the Americans dropped the atom bomb on my city. It was a hot, August morning and I had just heard on the radio that the Americans were planning an invasion of Japan. Our Emperor made a speech promising that we would never surrender and calling upon all 100 million people of the Japanese Empire to join together as a human shield to protect the Emperor and their country. We all knew what that meant. The week before I had been to the funeral of my friend's brother who died when his plane dive-bombed an American naval ship in the Pacific Ocean.

I was on my way to school when I heard a bomber flying overhead. I ran for cover. As I did so the buildings around me lit up with a bright pinkish light. I fell to the ground. Later I learned that anyone who had looked directly at the light had their eyes burned out. The bomb hit the centre of the city, which disappeared under a great mushroom cloud of smoke. Anyone within a kilometre of the explosion became a bundle of smoking black charcoal in seconds. In the first few minutes, 70,000 people were dead. Then came the blast wave, which destroyed 70,000 of the city's 78,000 buildings.

The following day we learnt that America had demanded our surrender – or they would drop another bomb. But before our Government could reply, a city further south was bombed – only three days later! On 14th August our leaders reluctantly surrendered. For the World, the war was finally over. But for us, the suffering continued. About three weeks after the bomb was dropped people who hadn't been injured at the time began to suffer a strange form of illness. The symptoms included vomiting, loss of appetite, purple spots on the skin, bleeding from the mouth and finally death. This became known as radiation sickness. The Americans, however, refused to admit it existed and banned journalists from reporting it. By 1950 the total number of people who had died from the bomb in my city had gone up to 200,000 and it's still rising.

Resource 3   **Examiner's Checklist**

The girl was 12 years old when the bomb was dropped			
It was on a hot August morning			
She listened to the Emperor's speech on the radio			
The Emperor asked the Japanese to protect him			
Her friend's brother died dive-bombing a US naval ship			
When the bomb was dropped there was a bright pink light which burned people's eyes out			
Within 1 kilometre of the explosion, people became a bundle of black charcoal			
In minutes 70,000 were dead			
70,000 out of 78,000 buildings were destroyed			
After the bomb was dropped America demanded Japan's surrender			
Three days later another city in the south was bombed			
On 14th August Japan surrendered			
Give one of the symptoms of radiation: vomiting, loss of hair, bleeding from the mouth, death			
America banned journalists from reporting about radiation sickness			
By 1950, 200,000 people had died from the effects of the bomb			

Student Learning Log

What was the purpose of the lesson?

What did you do?

What did you learn?

What did your teacher do to help you? (Tick as appropriate)

- [ ] explained the task
- [ ] told me what skills I would need
- [ ] gave instructions
- [ ] asked questions
- [ ] asked pupils to explain answers
- [ ] made me think
- [ ] made a comparison to other situations – give an example if you can

---

The lesson:

Was not interesting	1	2	3	4	5	Was interesting
Was not helpful	1	2	3	4	5	Was helpful
Made me think	1	2	3	4	5	Didn't really make me think
Was challenging	1	2	3	4	5	Was not challenging

Where else could you use these skills?

Exemplar 3

The Hundred Days

Context

Thinking Through History Strategies can assist older students in coping with the increased complexity and demands of advanced study.

I used this activity with my Year 12 class. The students had studied Napoleon's domestic and foreign policy in depth and we were coming up to look at The Hundred Days and his final abdication. The students had no previous knowledge of The Hundred Days (assuming they had not read ahead!) so I decided to use a different technique to go over the events. After several lessons 'led from the front', I wanted a lesson that would capture their imagination. My intended learning outcomes were:

- to make the students think;
- to give them some images to help them remember the events;
- to open up some alternative possibilities as a means to record and remember information;
- to access recording information according to the students' preferred styles of learning.

Preparation

Story-telling therefore seemed an ideal solution. The Hundred Days is by nature a good 'story', with plenty of dramatic events. The text is not too long but I made sure I was familiar with it and I even practised it out loud beforehand, as I believe you should read it at a normal pace.

Launching

After a brief question and answer recap on the events leading up to the Fourth Coalition and the Battle of Leipzig, I told the students they would need a piece of paper and a pen. Needless to say I was confronted with groans of *'Not another lecture, Sir!'* The activity requires no further 'scene setting' and as I wanted enough time for the debriefing I felt it was important to get straight into the activity.

Instructions

Very simply, I told the students that I was going to read them a story, at normal reading pace, and I wanted them to record what they could, in any way they felt necessary. It is important at this stage not to point them in any direction regarding how they record it: let them decide.

Managing the activity

This is a straightforward activity. The text should be read through by the teacher at a normal pace. It is important to give the students time at the end. I did not say anything until the last one had stopped writing, and it is even worth checking whether they need any more time. The next stage of the activity is the debriefing (see below). Then tell them you will read it over once more, but this time encourage them to use a fresh approach using any different techniques that have just been suggested. Read the story again and debrief this second attempt, before embarking upon any follow-up exercise.

Debriefing

Re-constructing the students' initial responses is worthwhile, as is eliciting alternatives for suggested improvements.

After giving them ample time to finish writing, I broke the silence by asking, light-heartedly, if anyone would like to repeat it word for word. Obviously no one did, so first we discussed who had found it hard (or easy) and why. Common responses included *'You read too fast'*, to which I always reply *'That's how I always read though'*. Or *'It was hard to keep up and get everything down'* and *'You can't write down what you said and listen at the same time'*.

The next stage in debriefing is twofold: to establish how they did it and how they could improve on it next time. Techniques suggested (to either question) were:

- using abbreviations;
- using bullet points;
- leaving gaps and coming back to them;
- selecting only the important bits;
- using drawings, symbols, figures or even maps;
- listening to all of it first then writing it down.

After considering the relevant benefits of each one, the students actually requested to repeat the exercise again, thus saving me the task of telling them. I encouraged them to try to take on board the advice, and use some of the techniques we had been discussing.

After giving them a fresh piece of paper, I read the story again. Once again, I gave them plenty of time at the end, and it was very noticeable that they all continued writing for at least two or three minutes after I stopped. I found this very encouraging, and told them so when they stopped writing. To debrief this second part of the activity, I asked them how they had done it this time, whether they thought it was easier, and whether they had recorded more this time. The responses were very positive. They had all taken on board some of the suggestions of others and they agreed they had managed to record far more. Most of them used bullet points and abbreviations but interestingly, one girl only wrote a few major points down and then went back and filled in the gaps. She said she pictured it as a chain of events and could easily go back and fill in the gaps. Even more remarkable was that one boy decided to record it all in diagram form. I persuaded him to hold it up. To the rest of us, the uninitiated, it looked a mess, but bit-by-bit, he described what each symbol meant and amazingly, he could recall virtually every single detail. It is always worthwhile choosing a couple of students to recount the story who you know have done well.

> The insights into improved 'study gains' acquired by the students' self-awareness of how they could organise their approaches to learning are often very significant, ie well worth the time spent 'away from the specifications'.

I also asked them if they could identify the skills they had used to attempt this task, which were:

- listening
- remembering
- visualising
- selecting
- sequencing
- explaining

Importantly, not only did all the students seem to enjoy the session, but they also saw it as worthwhile.

Finally, I posed the question *'In which situations might you find that recording information in different ways could be of value?'* The students suggested they could use such approaches *'in revision'* or *'in note taking in lessons'* or in *'note making from books'* or even *'when watching TV/video documentaries'*.

> A range of 'near transfer' opportunities.

Follow-up

The follow-up activity depends on time and course implications, and the inclination of the teacher. There will probably be twenty minutes left out of an hour's lesson (depending on the length of debriefing) and this could be effectively used for a brief storyboarding exercise (similar to the follow-up to *Exemplar 1*), which would improve selecting and sequencing skills as well as reinforcing their knowledge of the events. As many of my students like to have their work in neat written note form, another way you could follow up, especially if you have run out of time, would be to go over the story as a class at the start of the next lesson and the students could take notes from each other as they went. I did this too and was pleasantly surprised that they had remembered every single detail – and this, likewise, encouraged them.

> As with most memorable episodes, the benefits in relation to embedding and internalising the experience can produce surprisingly deep recollections within the students' long-term memories.

Story: The Hundred Days

After his abdication on 6th April 1814, Napoleon was taken to Elba where he was allowed to rule. He was provided with an annual pension of 2 million francs and a small army of 700 Imperial Guardsmen who volunteered to protect the island from pirates. His stay on Elba was made deeply unhappy by the refusal of the allies to allow him any contact with his son, the King of Rome. He was alarmed by rumours of allied plans to move him from Elba to the West Indies or the isolated volcanic island of St Helena. The final straw came when the Bourbons refused to pay the promised pension, leaving him to rely on the meagre resources of Elba for the upkeep of his soldiers and his small Court.

Napoleon had monitored the situation on mainland Europe carefully, and by the beginning of 1815 all the signs appeared favourable for an attempt to return to power. The allies, meeting in Vienna to redraw the map of Europe, were soon fiercely divided, the main conflict being over Poland. It seemed that war could break out among the allies at any moment. This was a situation that Napoleon knew only too well how to exploit. In France, the restored Bourbons soon made themselves unpopular. Conscription and tax increases introduced by Napoleon were unexpectedly retained. Although a liberal charter guaranteed constitutional rights, rumours of the restoration of confiscated Church and noble lands alienated both the middle class and the peasants.

The army felt the greatest resentment of all. In what appeared to be a calculated insult, the new King, Louis XVIII, immediately retired thousands of officers on half pay, their places taken by émigré royalists who, only months before, had fought against France. Worse still, thousands of angry and confused demobilised soldiers were stranded with little means of survival. The feelings of the rank and file gave Napoleon real hope that they would rally to him if he returned to France.

Faced with a choice between a bleak future on Elba and the opportunity for a return to power in Europe, Napoleon could not resist the urge to try his luck one more time. On 26th February 1815 he set sail in his one ship with the 1100 men of his personal escort. He landed at Antibes and marched for Paris. All along the route, whole army garrisons quickly abandoned their allegiance to the Bourbons and joined him. Marshal Ney (who had taken service with the Bourbons) was sent out to confront Napoleon at Lyons, but he too went over to his old commander. On hearing of Ney's defection, Louis XVIII fled, abandoning Paris to Napoleon.

Napoleon arrived in Paris to find the situation to his disadvantage. On hearing of his return, the allies had quickly patched up their differences. He was declared an international outlaw to be removed by allied military action. Before he could meet this external threat, however, he had to settle a troubled domestic scene and rally support.

Napoleon introduced a number of liberal measures, most probably to win popularity. Throughout The Hundred Days of his new regime, his main support seems to have come from the peasants, who viewed him as the guarantor of the land settlement, and from the army, whose soldiers had suffered so much at the hands of the Bourbons.

Napoleon could not spend long on domestic problems. The threat from abroad was too great. By the late spring of 1815, a British army under Wellington was assembling in Belgium with plans to link with a Prussian force under von Blucher. Behind them, Austria and Russia were mobilising in strength. As in the campaign of 1805, Napoleon realised the danger of allowing these allied armies the time to unite. He needed a quick victory: either to split the coalition, or force the allies to negotiate.

His attempts to organise an army were hampered by a lack of money and draught horses. Although he was helped by the return of prisoners of war, it was difficult to raise large numbers of troops because, right up until the start of June, he did not dare resort to conscription. Of the 300,000 men who were raised, many had to be used for border guard duties and internal policing against royalist uprisings. This left him with a striking force of 120,000 with which he unexpectedly marched into Belgium on 14th June 1815.

Napoleon's intention was to prevent Wellington's 90,000 men from linking up with von Blucher's army of 120,000, so that he could defeat them separately. He almost succeeded. On 16th June he defeated von Blucher's army at Ligny, although the Prussians were able to retire in good order because no enveloping force arrived.

The French now turned on Wellington. Napoleon mistakenly believed that the Prussians were no longer a threat, so he sent Marshal Grouchy after them with an army of 30,000 men. Grouchy never found von Blucher, who had kept in close contact with Wellington and was marching to join him at Waterloo.

The Battle of Waterloo, fought on 18th June 1815, was characterised by Napoleon's lack of energy and Ney's poor judgement. Rather than attempt any sort of manoeuvre, Napoleon simply planned to smash through the centre of Wellington's line using massed columns. When his plan was questioned by those present who had witnessed the steadiness of the British infantry in Spain, he swept their objections aside. He then passed tactical control of the battle over to Ney, who ordered a series of costly frontal attacks by infantry and unsupported cavalry. These crude French tactics almost succeeded, but when the Prussians unexpectedly arrived and attacked the French flank, Napoleon's army was routed.

Napoleon hurried back to Paris in the hope of raising yet another army, but this time the politicians refused to be cowed into obedience. Napoleon was forced to abdicate for a second time on 22nd June. He fled to the coast, hoping to escape to America or retire to England. But instead he was exiled to St Helena in the South Atlantic.

Community of Enquiry:
Philosophy through History

9 Community of Enquiry: Philosophy through History

Rationale

Developing your pupils' capacity to create, consider and communicate profound questions within a historical context – but not necessarily bound by it – lies at the heart of the Thinking Skills Strategy known as *Philosophy through History*.

At secondary level a good story retains its attraction to arouse pupils' interest and involvement. For these reasons stories can be an excellent device for stimulating and developing thinking in the classroom. If engaged by a story line, pupils will be better able to access its potential for their own thinking and learning. A story provides a real, meaningful context in which to explore key concepts: especially one that is accessible, and which may easily link with pupils' own experience inside or outside school. Often a story set in a contemporary context can be used as a powerful analogy to help pupils understand complex issues arising from the period being studied.

Exemplar 2
38 Witnesses offers one such example.

The three stories included here as Exemplars, were all used as a resource to create a **Community of Enquiry** – that is the whole class engaged in an exploration of ideas through discussion. After reading the story, the ideas, or questions to be discussed in depth are chosen by the pupils. It is they who decide what they think is important and where further enquiry is needed. This heightens motivation and interest as it gives them a crucial sense of ownership and part control of the 'learning journey'. Ways of achieving a **Community of Enquiry** in the classroom are discussed below. It is a very effective method of thinking since it benefits from the 'distributed intelligence' of the whole group.

This Strategy applies the principles behind 'Philosophy for Children' in terms of history-specific contexts.

Using stories in this way has three different aims:

- **Curriculum aims** – to help develop historical understanding as well as speaking and listening skills, particularly the development of discursive language.
- **Cognitive aims** – to develop thinking. This includes a number of important elements such as: questioning; defining; speculating; analysing; judging evidence; summarising.
- **Moral and social aims** – to develop students' confidence in their capacity to think for themselves; to encourage co-operation and respect for other people; to foster sincerity and open-mindedness.

The links between the moral issues raised, underpinned by the necessary classroom procedures and protocols, make aspects of the Strategy an ideal vehicle to teach citizenship requirements.

Stories could be used at different stages during the topic:

- **At the start of a topic** – to assess how much the pupils already know and to introduce them to some of the relevant issues. At this stage the discussions will be more informed by personal experience.
- **During a topic** – to help explain difficult concepts, to clarify the issues and problems facing people in the past and investigate the range of different attitudes, ideas and beliefs held.
- **At the end of a topic** – as a form of consolidation and review and to help pupils to make links and connections between different contexts across different areas of study.

The type of story to look out for is one that will generate questions of an open-ended, more 'philosophical' nature relevant to the (often moral) issues arising from the area of study. Poems (see *Exemplar 3*), film or documentary extracts, photographs and pictures, can all provide a focus for enquiry.

Although this Strategy is perhaps one of the most challenging to manage, it can also be one which leads to spectacular gains in terms of pupils' thinking. The Strategy outlined has had a successful pedigree within numerous first and primary schools, where teachers have built on the *Philosophy for Children* approach. (Lipman, 1993) Many children at the early years stage have successfully developed their thinking by using a similar approach through questioning characters facing situations in picture story books.

In some ways, the impact of this Strategy is immediate and tangible in terms of the high level of interest and motivation that it generates, and the climate of co-operation and tolerance that always seems to be created very swiftly. However, at first, it is not always easy to capitalise on this by implementing a questioning strategy that has a comparable impact on students' thinking. The amount of progress they make depends to an extent on the skill of the teacher as facilitator. It is a learning process for both, but with practice, students do make genuine strides that can be quite exhilarating to experience.

Managing the Strategy

Getting students involved in a genuine discussion on matters of interest and importance is not easy. Some ideas which have proved successful include:

- create a circular or 'conference-style' seating arrangement;
- get the class to establish and display their own discussion rules;
- allow the students at least part control of the discussion agenda;
- encourage the students to talk *to each other* – not always through you;
- get the students to face the speaker they are responding to;
- encourage the students to connect what they say with someone's previous comment by using the convention *'I agree/disagree with x because…'*.

The climate of co-operation and tolerance created in this way will generally create a context in which students can make real advances in the quality of their thinking. The difficulty for the teacher lies in knowing how best to intervene in the discussion and how often, so as to ensure that higher order thinking is achieved. The aim is to move the discussion away from anecdotal comment and unsupported observations to a style of discussion in which some or all of the following skills will be evident:

This represents a very helpful prompt list.

- **Reasoning** – logically supporting argument and judgements. *Why do you say that? Can you give me a reason?*
- **Defining** – clarifying concepts through making connections, distinctions and comparisons. *What do you mean by? Can anyone explain that? Is it always the case that…?*
- **Speculating** – generating ideas and alternative views through imaginative thinking. *Has anyone got another thought/idea/example? Who else can say something about it?*
- **Testing for truth** – judging evidence, examples and counter examples. *How could we tell if it was true? How do you/we know?*
- **Expanding on ideas** – sustaining and extending lines of thought and argument. *Who agrees/disagrees with x? Why? Can you say what you agree/disagree with?*
- **Self-correction** – revising a viewpoint in the light of an alternative or better supported argument. *Would you like to respond to what x has said? Do you think x has a point?*
- **Summarising** – abstracting key points or general rules from a number of ideas or instances. *Who can sum up what we have said? What are the ideas/arguments we have come up with?*
- **Being sensitive to different contexts** – what is specific to a given context? what is true of all contexts? *Is that always the case? Would you argue in the same way if…?*

Devising a questioning strategy that will help students develop these skills is not easy but comes with practice, trial and error!

Without doubt, the teachers' function in facilitating **Community of Enquiry** *demands a very difficult and challenging role.*

Adopting the role of a facilitator is surprisingly difficult to do. The students seem to recognise and appreciate the different role that the teacher is playing – and even the risk that this might involve:

'The teacher is on the same level… like a friend.'

'You were one of the group, followed our rules, and didn't cut in.'

'Your [the teacher's] opinion wasn't automatically going to be accepted.'

'You didn't dominate. You let people have their own opinions but gave them little boosts at different times by asking different questions.'

'I can see how it might be risky, you have to act like a friend but not lose respect… remain a teacher at the same time.'

Giving control of the agenda to the students, allowing yourself to be just 'one of the group', taking a directive approach to the discussion but not dominating it: all this is quite difficult to do. Particularly as most students are used to addressing every comment to the teacher and receiving an immediate teacher assessment of their response. However, if students are to develop their thinking abilities through thinking together, it's important to use your own opinions sparingly, and to withhold judgement by responding to student answers in a non-evaluative fashion. This can be done by calling on others to respond, for example by saying: *'Who agrees or disagrees with what x has said?' 'Who would like to respond?'*

> Nevertheless, with perseverance, the benefits are considerable, both to the teacher and equally to the pupils.

A note on preparation

Ideally, the classroom should be arranged so that all can see each other and the teacher. A circle of chairs or a conference-style seating plan is suitable. You may want to read the story yourself, or you may want to duplicate it for all the students to follow, possibly involving them in the reading. You will also need to give some thought to:

1 the possible discussion questions that the story may generate;
2 the sort of questions that you will ask to encourage students:
> to be clear in their thinking;
> to make thoughtful judgements based on reasons;
> and to develop their own views and explore and challenge the views of others.

> Worthwhile prerequisites to avoid the 'thinking on your feet' syndrome.

Adapting the Strategy

The Strategy used in all three Exemplars was to develop students' thinking by using stories to create a **Community of Enquiry**. One issue that has arisen from the use of this technique, is the amount of control to give the students over the discussion, if what they feel is important and worth further enquiry begins to conflict with the issues that the teacher feels are the most relevant and useful. It may be a concern that although students are developing their thinking abilities, they are straying away from the questions most likely to develop their *historical* understanding. Teachers could decide to use a ready prepared discussion plan and leading questions of their own devising. However, this may forfeit the high level of interest and motivation that allowing students ownership of the agenda inspires (see student comments above). A happy medium might be to ensure that both the teacher's and the students' agendas are met, if these are at variance. Often a judicious choice of reading material ensures that only relevant questions are likely to be asked, but students are constantly surprising!

> The dilemmas posed by this possible divergence of agendas are ones to consider.

Citizenship

Finally, it is also interesting to note just how many of the values and aptitudes fostered by the **Community of Enquiry** approach coincide with those elements soon to be required by the new citizenship curriculum. Examples include:

- practice of tolerance;
- courage to defend a point of view;
- willingness to be open to changing one's opinions and attitudes in the light of discussion and evidence;
- ability to make a reasoned argument;
- ability to co-operate and work effectively with others;
- ability to consider and appreciate the experience and perspective of others;
- ability to develop a problem-solving approach.

(From *Education for citizenship and the teaching of democracy in schools* Final report of the Advisory Group on Citizenship, 22 September 1998)

Thinking Through History

A Border Conflict

Context

This activity was taught in a middle school to pupils of mixed abilities in Year 8 (aged 12-13). The pupils were studying 'Britain 1500-1750', and this particular *learning from stories* Strategy was presented at the beginning of a Unit of work on 'The Unification of Britain'. The historical content, linked to the Strategy, was to investigate what society was like in the Anglo-Scottish borders prior to the Unification of the Crowns in 1603. It had a particular focus upon the unique social structure and lifestyle of the area, with particular reference to the law, and the way in which it was enforced.

This is an example of nesting a local issue within a national context.

Earlier in Key Stage 2, in their study of The Tudors in Year 5, the pupils had looked, briefly, at the 'border reivers' and their society. So, although this was some time ago, the groundwork had been laid. The topic of law and order was new to everyone, however.

The geographical location of the school, in Hexham, Northumberland is worthy of mention. I feel it was a significant factor in capturing the pupils' interest since many sites around the school and in the immediate locality experienced turbulent times, and the ancestors of many modern local families might well have been caught up in similar events.

Abstract concepts of loyalties, laws, and identities are given a concrete referant that pupils themselves can make sense of.

'In terms of the Key Stage 2 National Curriculum 2000:'

Skills, knowledge and understanding:

2a) Describe and explain the relationship between characteristic features of specified periods and societies including the experiences and range of ideas, beliefs and attitudes of people in the past.

2b) Consider the social, cultural, religious and ethnic diversity of the societies studied, both in Britain and the wider World.

2c) Describe, analyse and explain reasons for, and results of, the historical events, situations and changes in the periods studied.

Links to breadth of study:

History from a variety of perspectives: political, social, cultural.

Aspects of the history of England and Scotland.

Preparation

Arrange the classroom with a circle of chairs or conference-style. (see page 117)

Launching

We began by discussing the modern relationship between England and Scotland, especially in terms of national loyalties and feelings of national identities. It was very useful to refer to the on-going European Championship qualifying football matches between England and Scotland (or the Six Nations Rugby Union internationals) and discuss feelings about the Scots from a modern English perspective.

Instructions

I explained the format of the Strategy to the pupils, ie that I would read the pupils a story about a border incident concerning a hanging in a nearby town in 1587. Whilst listening to the story, I wanted the pupils to think of one or two questions, which would help them understand the story better. After the story we could select an interesting question which we could then develop into a class discussion.

Managing the activity

I read the story to the class. The pupils noted down one question based upon anything that they found interesting or puzzling about the story in terms of both factual detail or as a general issue. They were then asked to share their questions in pairs, and to discuss it and decide whether to put forward both questions to the whole class, or a joint effort. As pupils offered their questions, they were collected and recorded onto an OHP. The pupils' questions were as follows:

The story has many classic ingredients to 'hook' pupils' interests: heroes; villains; blood; crimes; and deaths.

What was a Warden?

What is a bastle?

What are kinsmen – is it the same as your family?

What is reiving?

Did the Scots really hate the English?
Why did they not want the English and Scots to get married?
What were the other things that they were not allowed to do?
Were the same families on both sides of the border?
Why was there all that fighting between England and Scotland?
Would the baby have been English or Scottish?
Did the laws change when England and Scotland joined up?
Is it right that the law or anybody else should dictate who you marry?
Should you be able to choose who to marry?

We then tried to sort out which were *factual* and which were *philosophical* questions, looking at the definition of these with reference to specific examples. Questions about factual details, eg *What is a bastle?* were put aside for further research at a later time.

Pupils then voted on two linked questions for detailed discussion. The first one chosen *'Why did they not want the English and Scots to get married?'* was not strictly a *philosophical* question in that it relates to a specific context, but was sufficiently open to elicit a range of views. The second one selected was more open-ended *'Is it right that the law, or anybody else, should dictate who you marry?'*

We also agreed on conventions for discussion. The class decided that we would use the device of prefacing each contribution with *'I agree with…'* or *'I disagree with…'* to encourage listening skills. We identified *'learning to listen'* as an important objective along with *'allowing everyone to be involved'*. This particular class can produce discussion of a very high level, but some pupils are very forceful and need to be reminded to let others have their say.

The discussion of the first question began with a number of general contributions about feelings towards the Scots and the apparent contradiction in the story between the attitude of the borderers and that of the authorities. Some teacher questioning was required to define the discussion, to focus on *why* the authorities were apparently so against cross-border marriages.

The Anglo-Scottish football rivalry was a useful analogy again and encouraged discussion of the problems of split loyalties: *'Who would you support, or fight for, if you had parents of both nationalities?'* They questioned the rights of the authorities to enforce such rules, which led into the second question. The second question engendered a very lively debate. Initially, all pupils were in favour of free choice of partner but someone introduced the idea of the problems of marriage between children of rival families. This led to parallels being drawn from a wide range of modern situations such as Northern Ireland and Kosovo, as well as Romeo and Juliet, and TV soap operas. Discussion also strayed into the problems of arranged marriages for religious reasons. Possibly it might have been better not to allow the discussion to become so wide ranging but they were so deeply involved that it was tempting to let them go!

Debriefing

After the discussion we compared its outcomes against our success criteria, ie listening to others and allowing everybody to be involved. In general pupils thought that listening skills were improved by using the *'I agree…'* convention, and that although it was a constraint on spontaneous thought (*'when you desperately want to say something you have to say 'I agree' – and you forget what you were going to say'*), it did force people to listen and consider others' views. The aim of *allowing everybody to take part* had partially been fulfilled, especially in the second part of the discussion, as philosophical questions such as this had no one correct answer and everyone could have a view (*'You don't have to be clever to say what you think'*). We still didn't get over the problem of the forceful characters, and agreed to work on conventions for limiting their contributions.

The story engendered great enthusiasm and provided a useful stimulus for further work. It was a situation with which many were familiar (in film and soap opera if not in real life) and with which they found it easy to empathise. This encouraged most of the group to tackle the research with enthusiasm, feeling that they wanted to know more. The story also provided an opportunity to explore and understand the attitudes of the authorities –

An interesting legalistic/philosophical question to focus upon.

Vital prerequisites to encourage active listening and turn-taking, and reinforce crucial key skills and those of social inclusion.

Positive signs of pupil involvement and **bridging** and **transfer** to analogous situations.

Helpful practice in de-constructing Key Skills: communisation; improving own learning.

A major step forward for those individuals with low self-esteem.

the monarchs on both sides operating through the Wardens – and how this affected the lives of people at lower levels of society. It also helped the pupils to understand the concept that England and Scotland were separate countries, and that this had far reaching consequences.

Follow-up

Using the factual questions that had been posed together with others raised in discussion, pupils researched the social and economic background of border society and the role of the Wardens. Less able pupils tended to concentrate on the descriptions: home, foods, weapons, bastle houses. More able pupils were encouraged to look at why things were as they were on the borders (geographical factors, attitude of the authorities) and at the differences between border society and conditions in other parts of the country. Using this they explored characters using role-play and 'hot seating', but could have produced a written account or a wall display. As a concluding activity they wrote up their account of the incident from the point of view of the Warden, including a description of the situation and reasons for the Warden's attitudes.

From here it was very easy to move on to discussing the 1603 Unification of the Crowns, the 1707 Act of Union and the effects that these had on cross-border relations.

> Throughout the exercise, the pupils enhanced their conceptual awareness and 'cashed-in' with reference to the historical context in a wide variety of possible outcomes.

The Hanging: a story told by Edward Fenwick, Haltwhistle, 1587

We all know what death is around here. We've had our fair share of raiding and killing. We have to, to survive. This vast open country is harsh: it frightens me sometimes, wondering where the next raid is coming from and if my cattle will be stolen. Although my bastle is well defended my kinsmen help when the raids come. The land is harsh, but Mary was lovely. I'd do anything for her. She was my only surviving child, and now the Wardens have hanged her. For what? Not blackmail, murder or reiving – but no. For love. Who am I? My name is Edward Fenwick, and Mary is – or was – my daughter. What did she do? I'll tell you...

The border's rotten. I'm told it's been worse. My dad told me about battles like Flodden, about the thousands of English and Scots who slaughtered each other, while he and his kin stripped the dead on the battlefield afterwards. He told me he didn't give a damn about the English and Scots – and that what matters is the name you had as a borderer. It's the same still: the people who matter most are the ones who stick by you. Not the Earls, not the ones in the big castles for the Wardens who are supposed to keep order. They'll shift with the wind. They look after themselves. They lay down the law. But we have laws of our own. Now Mary and Archie have paid the price for breaking the so-called rules. The crime? They fell in love.

Archie Graham was a young Scot. A lad we knew well. Outstanding – especially as he had this mop of red hair. Always larking about. A frequent visitor to our village, bringing cattle along the drove road south. A strong, well-armed lad, good to have on your side in a fight. But you should have seen his face when he looked at our Mary!

Mary was a real looker: golden hair and incredibly dark eyes. I'd spend a lot of my time keeping an eye on her whenever the young lads came round. But those two managed to give me the slip, and in the end I gave up wasting my energy. Perhaps I should have kept a tighter rein on her, but there's so much work to do looking after the beasts on the upland pastures and keeping the garden going, that it was impossible.

Of course I worried. She was a Fenwick and English, and he was a Scottish Graham. Not that it mattered to us round here. As

I've said, we respect the family groups more than we do the differences between English and Scots. But I did know the law and the law said that cross-border marriages should not happen.

But, the inevitable happened. My lass and Archie couldn't live without each other. When Mary realised that a bairn was on the way she told me everything. She told me that she and Archie would be married, that they would not have it any other way, and that she wanted him and the child more that anything else in the world.

What could I do? I scraped what little money I had together, and gave it to them with my blessing. It was nice to think of myself as a Granddad, as all our other children had died before they were five. The two of them went off over the border to live near Archie's family. I just hoped that they would get away with it – that we were too insignificant for the Wardens to bother with, but I was wrong. Time passed. They came to see me sometimes at night, so I kept in touch with them. They were so happy. We should have known better.

The blow fell shortly after the baby was born. The Warden's guards arrested them in Scotland, dragged them off to Court, and accused them of getting married without the Warden's permission. They were sentenced to be hanged, and me and my wife were forced to watch, there in the market place in Haltwhistle. I had to watch their bodies twitch, still suspended by the rope, long after they were dropped.

And what about the bairn? In my old age I have dreamed of a grandchild. I have made a little basket of thatched reeds. I have begun to make toys. I will look after him... He is all I have left.

Exemplar 2

38 Witnesses

Context

This story was used with a responsive, mixed ability Y9 group at the end of a 5-week cross-curricular project on the Holocaust. The question *'How did the Holocaust happen?'* had been the focus of their investigation in history lessons. The story was now intended to encourage students to reflect on some of the contributing factors and their relative importance, and to consider the lessons that can be drawn. The discussion was intended to help students review the topic and crystallise their ideas in preparation for a piece of assessed extended writing. The story was also supported by an extract from *Bystanders*, a BBC documentary from the *Modern Times* series.

> The Strategy can work equally well within a single-subject approach to the topic.

Preparation

Ideally, the classroom should be arranged so that all can see each other and the teacher. (see *Note on preparation* on page 118)

Launching

As the idea of using a story to create a **Community of Enquiry** was new to this class, its purpose was explained and it was presented as an experiment. Students were asked to consider the most disastrous discussion they had had as a class, and why it had been unproductive. Arising out of this, a set of rules was generated by the class, which they put on display and agreed to follow. They would judge their discussion by their own criteria at the end of the lesson. The rules they chose were:

> Establishing such 'rules of engagement' is a worthwhile preliminary phase.

- listen to what other people say and don't interrupt;
- don't say anything that is not relevant;
- show respect for other people's views;
- be patient and supportive when others are contributing;
- get involved.

They also agreed to begin each contribution with *'I agree/disagree with x because…'* This convention always has a positive effect. It helps to ensure that the first two criteria above are successfully achieved and encourages students to provide *supported* arguments and judgements.

Instructions

1. Before reading the story, tell the students that they will be given time afterwards to jot down any questions that come to mind as they listen.
2. Read the story and give the class some time to think before collecting comments and questions from individual students onto the board. (With a less responsive class, students could be asked to share their questions with a partner/small group before collectively offering a question for discussion with the rest of the class.)
3. Ask the class as a whole to vote on which question they want to discuss as a whole community.
4. Begin the discussion by inviting someone to respond to the question chosen.

> Be prepared, initially, for several 'thinking time' minutes from the pupils.

> At this stage avoid any temptation to 'bridge' across to the historical Exemplar – save it for later.

Examples of students' questions inspired by *38 Witnesses* include:

Do bystanders fail to act out of fear or indifference?
Are we indifferent to people we don't know?
Should we risk our own safety to help a stranger?
Is the bystander just as guilty as the perpetrator?

It is this type of open-ended question that stimulates the most fruitful discussion and has the most potential for developing students' thinking. Students themselves come to recognise this and with practice become more proficient at formulating questions of this kind.

Managing the activity

There is no doubt that the teacher's role in facilitating a **Community of Enquiry** is a complex and challenging one. (see *Managing the Strategy page 117*)

> This Thinking Skills Strategy is undoubtedly a challenging one. But one which, with practice, is achievable.

Debriefing

This was the group's first experience of building a **Community of Enquiry**, and their discussion was very successful in terms of the rules they had set for themselves. The discussion lasted for 35 minutes during which time no irrelevant comments, interruptions or put downs were made – this was quite an achievement for this particular class. During the debriefing session they were asked to articulate what had gone well and why. The key points that arose from this centred on:

- the value of agreeing rules in advance. *'The discussion was better because we actually planned it and made rules before we started. It's important that they were our rules.'*

- the climate of co-operation and tolerance that had been produced. *'People were willing to risk discussing their views and opinions.' 'You don't have to worry about being laughed at.' 'You hear other people reinforcing your view, saying they agree with you and why. This gives you a lot of confidence.' 'When people disagreed, they didn't argue but just expressed 'their' opinion. Nobody minded when there was disagreement as people picked reasons why they agreed and disagreed. This shows respect.'*

- the importance of giving control of the discussion agenda to the students. *'I liked it that the questions were ours not yours... it makes the discussion ours and you're more likely to speak and want to make it work.'*

They were also asked what they felt the importance of the story had been. Key points made focused on:

- the role that the story had played in generating interest. *'People concentrated because it was interesting... the story made it interesting from the start.'*

- how the story had made the lesson accessible for everyone. *'When you have an everyday example, everyone can give an opinion on this because you can more easily put yourself into the situation.'*

- the role of the story in helping students develop their historical understanding. *'The story put a picture in our minds which helped us think, and understand the situation we'd been studying.'*

The contributions of some students focused exclusively on the story or on their own experience. Most, however, moved beyond anecdotal comment and were able to discuss how the issues raised by the story could be applied to the historical context. Students were encouraged to draw on all their accumulated knowledge, but as the story focuses on the issue of bystanding, discussion specific to the Holocaust centred particularly on the following issues:

1 How big a factor is the astonishing human capacity for indifference to the plight of others in explaining the Holocaust? What is the role of fear?

2 How can we begin to evaluate the degree of responsibility of: ordinary Germans; the citizens of defeated and occupied countries; Germany's allies; the anti-Nazi Allies and finally the Jews themselves?

Most students appreciated the fact that the answers to their original discussion questions would be affected by the context. A few began to look for general rules that could be applied to all contexts.

> Note, the fusion of the 'what?' and the 'why?' together with 'how?'. The Strategy encouraged pupils to think through *how* they have learnt and *what* they have learnt.

> An especially effective phase. The pupils bridge to the historic context and transfer the moral dilemma – or do you assist them to do so?

38 Witnesses

For more than half an hour, thirty eight respectable, law-abiding citizens in Queens watched a killer stalk and stab a woman in three separate attacks in Kew Gardens. Twice the sound of their voices and the sudden glow of their bedroom lights interrupted him and frightened him off. Each time he returned, sought her out and stabbed her again. Not one person telephoned the police during the assault. One witness called after the woman was dead.

That was two weeks ago today. But Assistant Chief Inspector Frederick M Lussen, in charge of the borough's detective force and a veteran of 25 years of homicide investigations, is still shocked. He can give a matter-of-fact recitation of many murders. But the Kew Gardens slaying baffles him – not because it is a murder, but because the 'good people' failed to call the police. 'As we have reconstructed the crime,' he said, 'the assailant had three chances to kill this woman during the 35-minute period. He returned twice to complete the job. If we had been called when he first attacked, the woman might not now be dead.'

This is what the police say happened, beginning at 3.20am in the staid, middle-class, tree-lined Austin Street area:

28 year old Catherine Genovese, who was called Kitty by almost everyone in the neighbourhood, was returning home from her job as manager of a bar in Hollis. She parked her red Fiat in a lot adjacent to the Kew Gardens, Long Island, railroad station, facing Mowbray Place. Like many residents of the neighbourhood, she had parked there day after day since her arrival from Connecticut a year ago, although the railroad frowned on the practice. She turned off the lights of her car, locked the door and started to walk the 100 feet to the entrance of her apartment at 8270 Austin Street, which is in a Tudor-style building with stores on the ground floor and apartments on the first. The entrance to the apartment is in the rear of the building because the front is rented to retail stores. At night the quiet neighbourhood is shrouded in the slumbering darkness that marks most residential areas.

Miss Genovese noticed a man at the far end of the lot, near a seven-storey apartment house at 8240 Austin Street towards Lefferts Boulevard, where there is a call box to the 102nd Police

Precinct in nearby Richmond Hill. She got as far as a street light in front of a bookstore before the man grabbed her. She screamed. Lights went on in the ten-storey apartment house at 8267 Austin Street, which faces the bookstore. Windows slid open and voices punctured the early morning stillness.

Miss Genovese screamed 'Oh, my God, he stabbed me! Please help me!' From one of the upper windows in the apartment house, a man called down 'Let that girl alone!'. The assailant looked at him, shrugged and walked down Austin Street toward a white sedan parked a short distance away. Miss Genovese struggled to her feet. Lights went out. The killer returned to Miss Genovese, now trying to make her way around the side of the building by the parking lot to get to her apartment. The assailant stabbed her again. 'I'm dying!' she shrieked. 'I'm dying!' Windows were opened again, and lights went on in many apartments. The assailant got into his car and drove away. Miss Genovese staggered to her feet. A city bus, Q10, the Lefferts Boulevard line to Kennedy International Airport, passed. It was 3.35am. The assailant returned. By then, Miss Genovese had crawled to the back of the building, where freshly painted brown doors to the apartment house held out the hope of safety. The killer tried the first door. She wasn't there. At the second door, 8264 Austin Street, he saw her slumped on the floor at the foot of the stairs. He stabbed her a third time, fatally.

It was 3.50am by the time the police received their first call from a man who was a neighbour of Miss Genovese. In two minutes they were at the scene. The neighbour, a 70-year-old woman, and another woman were the only persons on the street. Nobody else came forward. The man explained that he had called the police after much deliberation. He had phoned a friend in Nassau County for advice, and then he had crossed the roof of the building to the apartment of the elderly woman to get her to make the call. 'I didn't want to get involved' he sheepishly told the police...

Taken from *38 Witnesses*
The New York Times Company, 1964.

Exemplar 3

The intention behind this Strategy was for pupils to revisit recurring themes and allow pupils to create new layers of knowledge and understanding by making explicit links and connections.

Many of the messages within *Exemplars 1* and *2* also apply to this Exemplar.

Circles

Context

This poem was used with the same Y9 group, 4 months later, at the end of a Unit of work on the Indigenous Peoples of North America. Within the topic, the students had investigated how stereotypes of the Native Americans had arisen, researched in depth the life and culture of the Plains Indians and then used their knowledge and understanding to evaluate some of the different ways in which the Plains Indians have been represented in a variety of documents, paintings, photographs and feature films (from the sixteenth to the twentieth century).

The poem was intended to generate discussion that would help students consolidate what they had learned and reflect on the causes of intolerance and racism. One particular aim was that they should begin to make connections between different contexts across different areas of study, eg comparing and contrasting the reasons for racial intolerance towards Native Americans in nineteenth century America, and the Jews in Hitler's Germany.

Preparation

Give some thought to the classroom arrangement and the discussion which might take place. (see *Rationale*, page 116)

Launching

The idea of using a poem, story or other resource to create a **community of enquiry** was no longer new to this group. They had by now experienced the technique a few times so launching the activity was relatively easy. They were given time to review what had gone well on past occasions and why as well as what needed improvement and whether they wanted to amend any of their original discussion rules.

Instructions

1 Before reading the poem, tell the students that they will be given time afterwards to jot down any questions that come to mind as they listen.

2 Read the poem and give the class some time to think before collecting comments and questions from individual students onto the board. (With a less responsive class, students could be asked to share their questions with a partner/small group before collectively offering a question for discussion with the rest of the class)

3 Ask the class as a whole to vote on which question they want to discuss as a whole community.

4 Begin the discussion by inviting someone to respond to the question chosen.

On this occasion, however, before offering their questions for discussion, the students were asked to think about the 'message' of the poem in pairs. They then rephrased their ideas into question form. This intermediate step seemed to make it easier for some students to formulate the type of open-ended, more 'philosophical' questions that have the most potential for developing students' thinking.

Examples of students' questions inspired by the poem Circles include:

'Why are people racist?'
'Will intolerance and racism always exist?'
'What does it mean to be knowledgeable?'
'What's the difference between knowledge and wisdom?'
'Is knowledge really what makes a person 'greater'?'
'Is it possible for one person to be 'greater' than another?'

Debriefing

A major step forward in many pupils' thought processes.

On this occasion more emphasis was placed in the debriefing session on getting the students to reflect on the quality of their thinking and the skills they thought they were acquiring through the use of this technique. There seemed to be a consensus in the group that they were becoming *better thinkers*. All were confident that they could recognise 'good reasoning', and although it was difficult to do, they appreciated its value. There was lots of comment about the importance of being prepared to revise a viewpoint when confronted with inconsistencies in your own argument:

Thinking Through History

'Before I would say: well that's just my opinion and you can't take it away from me. I didn't think about why I thought it. But I can see it's not worth much unless you can give a good reason.'

'You have to give a good reason if you want people to take you seriously.'

'It teaches you to be open minded… to be prepared to change your view… there's lots of agreement and disagreement throughout the class… so it's OK to back down.'

Some students commented on the value of the **Community of Enquiry** approach:

'What you learn that's valuable is respect… listening to other people… being open minded.'

'It brings the class together.'

'It makes you more reasonable.'

'You get time to think.'

On this occasion the questions, chosen by the group, began to move the discussion away from the intentions outlined in the *Context* section above. This problem is discussed earlier under *Managing the Strategy*. (see page 117)

Follow-up

Follow-up activities could include:

1 Filling in 'thought bubbles' from both the White American settler and Native American point of view. To facilitate this, students could be given a framework of questions to answer from both perspectives, drawing on their knowledge of the clash of beliefs, lifestyle and culture between the two:

> *'What does x believe?'*
> *'What does x fear?'*
> *'What does x want?'*
> *'What reasons would x give?'*
> *'What does x think that y should do?'*

> These possible follow-ups offer a range of motivating activities which are accessible, active and inclusive for all pupils regardless of their abilities.

2 The 'thought bubbles' could lead in to role-play where students act out a more detailed discussion between the two characters, exploring the nature of their differences more thoroughly.

3 Alternatively, the teacher or individual students could act in role as one or other of the characters and answer questions from the group, 'hot seat' style.

4 Although not suited to this particular poem, another idea that works well with a story set in historical time, is to ask the class to create, in small groups, a frozen image of a moment in the story that has particularly struck them. When tapped on the shoulder, individual students must reveal their 'hidden thoughts'. This again, encourages students to identify with different characters in the story and to see a situation from different perspectives.

Circles

*The white man drew a small circle in the sand
and told the red man*

*'This is what the Indian knows' and drawing a
big circle around the small one*

'This is what the white man knows'

*The Indian took the stick and swept an immense
ring around both circles*

*'This is where the white man and the red man
know nothing'*

Carl Sandberg

Professional Development

10 Professional Development

It was stated in the *Introduction* that this book can be used at a variety of levels. If *teaching thinking* is to make a significant contribution to your department or school then professional development has to be seriously addressed. A number of curriculum development projects have come to the same conclusion: *'There is no curriculum development without teacher development'*.

The model below was developed through the research on *Effective Teachers of Numeracy* (Askew et al, 1997) and provides a very useful vehicle for both understanding professional development issues and how they can be pursued. Being a model, it inevitably simplifies reality.

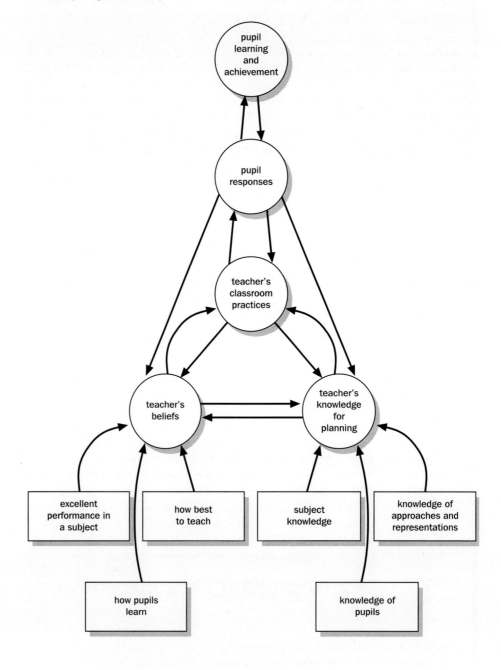

Arrows indicate potential positive development

**A model to explain development of effective practice
(after Askew et al, 1997)**

The model suggests that effectiveness develops through the interaction of knowledge about teaching one's subject (pedagogical content knowledge – or PCK), beliefs about teaching and pupils' learning, classroom practice and pupils' response to classroom practice. One can map the use of this book and its approach onto that model. First, it will be assumed that your beliefs about teaching are in general alignment with *teaching thinking*. One could categorise this book as 'knowledge of approaches', which will have a positive impact on your PCK and perhaps reinforce your beliefs. You plan the lesson based on your understanding of the material in the book, and you deliberately alter your practice to some degree, perhaps by reinforcing the concept that there is no one correct answer, but pupils have to have reasons for their responses. The pupils really get into it and enjoy both the task and giving their ideas and reasoning. Their response is positive, therefore, and this has feedback effects on your practice, your knowledge (PCK) and your beliefs. However, your attempts at asking pupils about how they have done the task meet with blank looks and silence. This may discourage that part of your attempts to implement change. Now, let's switch to a teacher who, by virtue of their beliefs is less open and sympathetic to *teaching thinking*. Their PCK, and by implication their planning, does not alter. They introduce the **Mystery** without much thought or attention. The pupils are confused by the unfamiliar demands, and some play up. The feedback to this teacher is negative and there is no impetus or energy that will drive the development of their thinking or practice. The attempt at change will peter out, and the status quo will resume. *'I'm not doing that again, it doesn't work'* could be the teacher's summative comment. Professional development opportunities and resources are required to encourage teachers to go as far as they can with *teaching thinking*. You may need help to develop your debriefing skills. The more reluctant teacher may need help in planning the delivery and management of the task. Should the reluctant teacher be pressurised? Although this is a moral question we can give three reasons why they might be. Firstly, teachers are accountable and this is a form of support that will help meet such demands. Secondly, pupils deserve and need a degree of challenging and stimulating teaching. Thirdly, we do not know any teachers who have achieved a level of competence in *teaching thinking* who do not enjoy it – and believe that the majority of their pupils enjoy it.

The five points listed below can all be related to the *Effective Teachers of Numeracy* model. Based on the experience of the Thinking Through Geography Group and the Teacher Training Agency-funded North East School Based Research Consortium (NESBRC), we strongly commend the following:

1 If you get the active support of your senior management team (SMT) then the environment for the curriculum and pedagogical change will become supportive: in a sense it pervades the white background of the model. Put *teaching thinking* in your Departmental Development Plan and relate it to an issue in the School Development Plan. Raising Attainment, Boys' Underachievement or Disaffection, Teaching and Learning Styles, Active or Accelerated Learning, Literacy, Citizenship, Target Setting are all among the range of headings to which Teaching Thinking can be linked. Keep the SMT informed: identify a member of the SMT who is particularly supportive and get that person to attend a departmental meeting, look at your materials, observe a lesson or go on a course. Remind the SMT, if necessary, that what you are doing is part of the NC. Use the SDP to get a share of school funds to take *teaching thinking* forward.

2 Put some thought into how you will take it forward as a department. On the assumption that you are the Head of Department or that she/he is sympathetic, set a goal that everyone in the department teaches a particular *thinking* lesson with a particular year group, and then compares notes. Try then to build on this by perhaps having a *thinking* lesson every half term, and use the successes of individuals to set the benchmarks for the whole department.

3 There are many benefits to undertaking some action research into *teaching thinking*. Action research can help you develop your thinking, planning and classroom practice, and gives wonderful insights into pupils' thinking, learning, self-concepts and attitudes. Some obvious forms of data collection are:
   • video-recording a lesson with some focus on teacher inputs and some on pupils' talk and work in groups;

- getting pupils to keep learning logs addressing such questions as 'What did you learn in that lesson?', 'What existing knowledge did you use and how did it help?' and 'What did the teacher do that helped you learn?'
- interviewing pupils about how they did a task: how did they start? how did their strategies change? what ideas, images or previous knowledge informed their work? how did they operate as a group? what kind of help do they find useful? is this teaching different? has this teaching changed their ideas about the subject, school, education, learning, jobs etc?
- analysing pupils' written work to identify what more successful pupils are doing that less successful pupils are struggling with (diagnostic assessment).

4 Collaboration with networks of other teachers. This could be with like-minded teachers from your school: does the school use CASE (a science intervention)? or CAME (maths)? do the geographers use *Thinking Through Geography* materials? Or, it could be in an LEA subject network or through a higher education course. 24-hour residentials which include viewing videos of *teaching thinking* lessons have proved particularly powerful and popular in North East England.

5 Coaching is an emergent and highly promising form of professional development. Coaching is more focused and specific than mentoring or appraisal and is not connected to power or promotion: it is about developing particular teaching behaviours. In the NESBRC and CASE networks in Northern England, coaching has proved to be very effective both for the coach and the coached. At a simple level you can do this in your own department. Or talk to your adviser or your SMT about organising some coach training. Pressure from below can sometimes force change.

For a fuller treatment of some of the issues facing individual teachers in trying to implement *teaching thinking* read *Rolling the Stone Uphill*. (Leat, 1999)

Curriculum Development

This part of the book is written for those who wish to go further than just using the materials or adapting the Strategies to other contexts (Levels 1 and 2, see *Introduction*, page 6). If you want to start building *thinking* into the history curriculum and perhaps into the whole curriculum (Levels 3 and 4) then read on.

The work on *teaching thinking* centred on Newcastle University has been stimulated by a number of factors:

1 The National Curriculum has had the unfortunate effect of making teachers play safe and cover content. There has been some tendency to teach the nouns (the content) in the PoS with much less attention to the verbs (the processes).

2 Many pupils leave school underachieving. Whilst a Grade D, E, F or G at GCSE may represent a great effort by a pupil and her/his teacher, it is a sad reflection on 11 years of compulsory schooling. Many able pupils do well at GCSE, but without becoming good learners – and they really struggle thereafter. We have the ambition to see more pupils doing better.

3 Many teachers are really motivated by *teaching thinking*. It reawakens their interest in teaching because it shows pupils in a new light. Thus it is a wonderful vehicle for professional development for PGCE students, Newly Qualified Teachers, Subject Leadership and, in some contexts, Performance Management.

There is a need for a reappraisal of the whole curriculum, which is partly reflected in *The Curriculum 2000* with its references to Key Skills, Thinking Skills and Citizenship. Instead of trying to produce a curriculum that most pupils can cope with, there is a strong case for BUILDING A CURRICULUM THAT CHANGES THE LEARNER, so that pupils do become more effective learners who are well equipped for the demands of further and higher education and the workplace. The Strategies are not only aimed at less successful pupils, they are also highly suitable for the gifted and talented. We do not pretend that reshaping the curriculum is easy, but it is ultimately satisfying.

Curriculum Design Principles

It is very hard to explain exactly how materials and strategies develop. It is partly a magical process that might be attributed to intuition or creative thinking. However, we can be clear about some of the principles that have underpinned the approach to turning good ideas into successful materials and activities in the classroom. Some of these principles may appear a bit theoretical, but stick with it. Theoretical has become a dirty word in some quarters, but as the saying goes 'there is nothing as practical as a good theory'. Teachers involved in the *teaching thinking* subject networks have found that not only can they produce theory from their practice but that their thirst for using other research is created by their engagement with action research in their classrooms.

1. Constructivism. In simple terms constructivism implies that we learn through what we already know. When we say 'That makes no sense to me' we usually mean 'I have no mental resources to understand what I have seen or been told.' If someone from Britain listens to a radio commentary on a tennis, football or cricket match they will stand a good chance of understanding what is going on. If on the other hand we listen to a commentary on American football, hurling (Irish) or sumo wrestling, most of us are struggling (despite the best efforts of the TV company). This is because few of us have much experience of these sports, so we do not have a mental framework through first hand experience, and appropriate language to interpret what is being said. It is not the fault of the commentator: it is that we do not have an adequate receiver to interpret the words. So it is with pupils in many lessons: they do not have the mental frameworks to understand what is being delivered.

Many teachers already take account of this through their use of analogies, examples and stories. You use some knowledge that pupils already have to help them understand something new. The much quoted teacher aphorism 'Start where the pupils are at' is an expression of constructivism.

It is suggested that if new information can be interpreted through existing knowledge structures, termed schema (plural schemata), then it will be incorporated into a better understanding of a topic. If no connection can be made with existing knowledge then the new information will be lost – as water off a duck's back (notice the use of analogy). It is hypothesised that there is a very productive and important mid-point between these conditions: where some connection is made but where there is a degree of mismatch between the incoming and the established knowledge. This is termed **cognitive conflict** and is associated with the formation of new concepts. Just occasionally, we get a small window on this happening for a pupil, when they might say, with feeling '*Ahh – I get it!*'

If one accepts the above, then it should be understood that because everyone has somewhat different experiences and powers of perception, then every individual constructs their own unique understanding of the world. If you do happen to have spent months training to be a sumo wrestler then you are better equipped to learn more about it.

So how does this idea of constructivism help? It is incredibly hard, and probably unrealistic, to gauge the existing understanding of every pupil, so:

- On some occasions you can encourage pupils to access their existing knowledge, and try to make it available for them to construct new understanding. **Reading Photographs** and **Lifelines** are obvious examples of this, but brainstorming is another, especially where one is asking pupils what they already know.

- Providing experiences for pupils through which they might understand a new topic or idea. This may be through demonstrations, analogies, simulations etc. Such activities will often form part of the *launching* stage in a *thinking* lesson: giving activities to pupils in which they can actively try new information against understanding they may already have. **Mysteries** are an example of this.

For a short introduction to constructivism, the introductory chapter of *Making Sense of Secondary Science* (Driver, Squires, Rushworth & Wood-Robinson, 1994) serves well. But for a more thorough treatment, read '*How Children Think and Learn*' (Wood, 1988) or '*The Child as Thinker*'. (Meadows, 1993)

2. Metacognition. Don't get frightened by the word. In simple terms, metacognition means 'thinking about thinking' in such a way that one has a conscious awareness of it. It correlates with being less impulsive, and being more inclined to tackle a task or problem intelligently. If you have a troublesome teenage daughter or son and they are winding you up, you get cross and give them a verbal blast, and this develops into a row, you have been fairly impulsive. If on the other hand you think for a moment 'Hm... this is annoying, but I think she is doing this because she needs to establish her identity and independence, so it would probably be better if I...' then you are being metacognitive. (but you may not be any more successful with your troublesome offspring.) If a pupil, when faced by a historical issue or problem, asks herself 'What is this about? What have I done before that can help me?' then she is using metacognition. One of the keys to developing metacognition with pupils is developing a language for discussing their thoughts and strategies. Generally as teachers we are not well equipped for this task. Many people are surprised by the level of sophistication pupils can achieve in thinking about thinking. It is through debriefing that metacognition is developed. For further reading on metacognition, try Brown (1987) and von Wright (1992).

3. Challenge. The short term aim of the Strategies in this book is to challenge pupils, to provide a rich learning environment in which they have to think hard. (the term cognitive conflict has been used to describe this.) This has to be done carefully. There is no point in giving pupils work that is way beyond their capabilities. As a benchmark, it is educationally healthy to give pupils activities which are just beyond their present capabilities, so that they have to struggle. (think how very young children are always trying to do things that are too difficult!) The Russian psychologist Vygotsky developed the concept of the **Zone of Proximal Development**, which is represented by the difference between what a pupil can do on their own and what they can do supported by more able peers or adults. As teachers we should be trying to move pupils through their ZPD, helping them to do independently what they can presently do with the assistance of others. This calls for a diagnostic approach to assessment in which one is constantly pursuingthe identification of present and potential performance – and trying to close the gap. (see the report on assessment *'Inside the Black Box'* by Black & Wiliam, 1998.)

However, what pupils can do is highly dependent on their motivation. If they have good self esteem they will tackle most things. It follows therefore that with lower sets one needs to establish a good relationship, in which they trust you and where you are supportive of their efforts and reinforce their successes. This makes an absolutely fantastic difference to what pupils are prepared to try.

As a teacher you can do a great deal for pupils to help and encourage them to undertake challenging tasks:

- by using explanations, demonstrations, stories and analogies, you can make sure that that they have an initial purchase on the relevant concepts, skill and language that they need;
- by building confidence and valuing and reinforcing what you see as important in their continued learning – such as listening;
- by using the more able within the class to support the learning of the less able. (this has to be done sensitively as some more able pupils resent it.)

A generic term used to describe this process is **scaffolding**.

4. Talk and Group Work. From the above it should be no surprise that talk both between pupils and between pupils and teachers is fundamental to this approach. It is through language that we achieve much of our learning. There is a phrase 'talking oneself into meaning'. Almost certainly you have had the experience of talking to someone and they (or you) say 'Now I get it' or 'I see what you mean' or 'Do you mean that ...'. Understanding develops through talk as ideas and interpretation are communicated and shared.

Most of these Strategies are best employed through group work. Some research shows that group work is not successful as a learning environment, but in these instances it is almost certain that pupils are doing the same task around a table but with no co-operative learning endeavour: they are working *in* groups, rather than *as* groups. (Galton, Simon & Croll, 1985)

The National Oracy Project provided some markers that are a useful indication of the quality of talk:

1 **Reciprocity.** Do pupils respond to and build upon what each other says, or are they like separate radio stations broadcasting on their own wavelength and not receiving? Good talk in groups should be collaborative, as the strengths and weaknesses of different ideas are considered from different perspectives, leading to the acceptance of the better ideas and solutions. (Kruger, 1993)

2 **Speculation, making connections and interpreting.** One report from the National Oracy Project developed these categories of pupil talk (D'Arcy, 1989), with the suggestion that speculation might be the most highly prized function of talk. 'What if?', 'perhaps', 'I wonder', 'maybe if they...' are all snippets that we should be pleased to hear.

3 **Pupils talking at length.** Research from Britain and the US suggests (eg, Sarason, 1982) that in most whole class discussions the teacher is the main talker, and pupils rarely get to speak for more than 2 seconds. A question is asked, the pupil gives a short answer (perhaps one word) and then the teacher finishes off the exchange, almost putting words in their mouths. Pupils speaking for 10 seconds can be a good benchmark of change.

4 **Pupils initiating.** Again, depressing evidence abounds to show that there is a consistent pattern to classroom talk. The teacher **initiates**, the pupil **responds**, and the teacher **evaluates** (IRE). (Sinclair & Coulthard, 1975) Pupils rarely initiate. These activities are designed to encourage pupils to initiate: as they are challenged, and begin to speculate!

5 **Teacher questions.** Most teacher questions are closed recall questions 'What weapons did Roman soldiers use?', 'Who were the Luddites?', 'How many British troops were killed and wounded on the first day of the Battle of the Somme?' etc. If pupils are to be encouraged to speculate and feed back their interpretation (construction of meaning) then the teacher needs to ask more open questions. Closed questions still have their place, however. These activities positively encourage the asking of *open* questions.

There is a great deal of skill in managing group work, some of which comes out in the sections on implementing the Strategies (see *page 8*), but more can be found elsewhere (see for example Stanford, 1990). Group composition requires some thought, but where possible mixed ability groups are desirable because of the value that variety brings. The less able can be supported by the more able; the more able learn from explaining and interpreting. Furthermore, there are many pupils who are not brilliant at written work but who are stars in groups and vice versa. Friendship groups have some advantages but they may agree on solutions too easily.

One of the most significant issues in *teaching thinking* activities is when to intervene in a group. It can be very destructive to go up to a group and say 'How are you getting on?' as it can break their flow and it may take them a long time to get back to their discussion. There is a tendency for us to feel that we are not doing our job if we are not interacting with pupils. As a general rule DO NOT INTERRUPT GROUPS IF THEY ARE WORKING WELL, even if this is tempting. Instead, try to listen to what groups are saying so that you can draw upon their thoughts and insight in the debriefing stage.

For further reading on the importance of small group talk see Sharan (1980) and Wood (1980). Two excellent general texts are *'Thinking Voices: the Work of the National Oracy Project'* (Norman, 1992) and *'Words and Minds: How we use Language to Think Together'* (Mercer, 2000).

5. Second Order Concepts and Cognitive Strategies. We believe that it is helpful to conceive of history in terms of a number of central underpinning concepts, through which much subject matter is understood. Pupils find this helpful. Otherwise the subject becomes a mass of rather disconnected content. There is a wonderful quote from a sixth former about science '*Science was a load of rubbish. One day you will come in and cut up a bull's eye and the next day you will come in and they will tell you what salt was. It was absolute rubbish, it didn't teach you nothing.*' (Ebbutt & Watts, 1987)

All subjects are open to the same accusation. Nichol (1998, page 39) distinguishes seven structural concepts in history:

'*Change*
Continuity
Cause
Consequence
Chronology
Situation
Evidence'

'*Central to history is the study of* change *and* continuity. Causation *examines why things change or remain unaltered.* Consequence *deals with the outcomes of change.* Chronology *places related data in a temporal dimension.* Situation *provides a physical location.* Evidence *addresses the evidential nature of the discipline. Organisational concepts provide analogies for defining events and movements in different periods. Terms such as feudalism, revolution, capitalism and imperialism are generically used. They draw their specific meaning from their contexts, for example the French and Russian Revolutions. Specific concepts relate to particular periods, and enable us to make sense of events within them.*'

Nichol also stresses the importance of cognitive strategies, which he lists as:

'*Gathering and organising – questions and questioning*
Recognising and defining
Generating
Planning
Monitoring and checking
Evaluating
Transferring and generalising
Communicating'

To an extent the detail of the list does not matter. What matters is that you have a list that you share with pupils so that they can understand and use them across a wide variety of contexts. It is our experience that this approach works extremely well. The concepts, skills and strategies are made visible through the debriefing process.

6. Bridging and Transfer. It is the assumed aim of education that what pupils learn in one context they will be able to transfer to and use in another. The evidence is largely to the contrary.

In the *launching* and *debriefing* sections of some of the Exemplars, therefore, we are at pains to give attention to **bridging**. In general terms the teacher encourages the students to see connections between what they have done and learned in particular lesson(s) and other contexts. These contexts may be in other Units of work in history, or in geography or science or, best of all, in the contexts of their own lives.

If pupils are successful in using what has been learned in one place they can be said to have **transferred** their learning. (Blagg, Ballinger & Lewis, 1993) If the context is fairly similar it is termed 'near' transfer and if the context is very different from the original it is termed 'far' transfer. Bridging by the teacher may be seen as part of the multiplier factor in taking the learning from an exciting, challenging and enjoyable lesson and making it count in the intellectual development of the pupil. Pupils tend to regard work as synonymous with writing. It takes a considerable effort to remove these constraints and blinkers, derail the production line mentality and get pupils to see the recurring patterns in the world.

For further reading see Perkins & Salomon (1988).

7. Accelerated Learning. The work of Alastair Smith (1996) on **accelerated learning** has proved very popular with teachers in recent years. *Teaching thinking* is very compatible with this approach. This can be achieved by offering pupils a variety of stimulus formats, so that they can learn by looking (at photographs – see **Reading Photographs**), using their imagination and own experience **(Mind Movies)**, talking **(Mysteries)** and listening actively and retelling narratives **(Story-telling).** Further, Gardner's Multiple Intelligences are well catered for. *Teaching thinking* actively employs pupils' existing knowledge and provides a 'big picture' within which to locate their learning outcomes, both procedures central to accelerated learning.

8. Thinking Skills and Other Agendas. Thinking skills approaches do not constitute a whole curriculum in the broadest sense – they are not a complete panacea to all educational ills (however enthusiastic we may be). There are four points we would like to stress in relation to this:

1   You may be highly successful in motivating and challenging your pupils. They become more thoughtful and begin to understand history through the second order concepts which they start to use in unfamiliar contexts. For some pupils, however, there may still be a major barrier to achievement in poor literacy, which may seriously handicap them in examinations. If cognitive acceleration becomes a whole-school issue, then a complementary programme to tackle poor literacy may be essential. (See for example Lewis & Wray, 1997 for more on Writing Frames and Christine Counsell, 1997 on Analytical and Discursive Writing)

2   *Teaching thinking*, when coupled with debriefing, provides critical feedback to pupils on their reasoning. This accords with the principles of formative assessment identified by Black & Wiliam (1998) who have demonstrated that this approach can improve GCSE results by between 1 and 2 grades. *Teaching thinking* can take assessment onto a completely new plane, a topic, however, which is beyond the scope of this book.

3   Don't forget what you are already good at. Teachers who use thinking skills are not meant to be clones. Effective use may require some changes in classroom practice, but hang on to the things that make you good anyway. This could be good relationships, high expectations, reward systems, setting targets, good display work, using topical events or using drama techniques. These can all happily weld on to the changes implicated here in a productive synergy.

4   Review your work. If resources allow this could include video recording lessons or getting pupils to complete questionnaires or learning logs. At a more mundane level keep watching and listening as this feedback will fuel your understanding of learning, which must underpin long term planning. Where possible plan and review with your colleagues from your school or from others so that you can benefit from collaborative learning.

Devising Curriculum Units

Clearly the step beyond using individual Strategies is to consider using the principles outlined above to infuse *teaching thinking* into schemes of work. We can offer the following pointers for this process:

1   Be clear about the second order concepts that you are trying to develop.

2   Use the Strategies as a checklist for ways in which students can be challenged and in which concepts can be developed.

3   Try to include explicit opportunities for pupils to develop skills listed in the NC Thinking Skills and Key Skills. An economical approach is to use a particular Strategy three or four times during a year and target particular skills that the Strategy requires. Specify the nature of progression you are planning for and try to find a way in which it can be assessed, perhaps through pupil self assessment or peer assessment.

4   Plan and use debriefing sessions in which you encourage the development of transfer, particularly by offering other contexts to which the students' learning can be applied.

Action Research

Finally it is worth pointing out that the design of *teaching thinking* materials and the process of trialling and evaluating them is ideal territory for action research. (Elliott, 1991) You research your teaching with the intention of improving some aspect of your practice. *Teaching thinking* has stimulated a lot of applications for DfES Best Practice Research Scholarships, which indicates that it gets people excited.

Bridging, Transfer and Debriefing

When a teacher suggests that the learning from one lesson can be used in another context, it is termed bridging. Mayer & Wittrock (1996, p48) define transfer as *'when a person's prior experience and knowledge affect learning or problem solving in a new situation'*. Essentially teachers engage in bridging so that pupils might transfer. *Teaching thinking*, as a pedagogy, is founded on a belief that pupils' learning in lessons can affect learning in other contexts. A distinction is sometimes drawn between near and far transfer, which denote the degree of similarity between the original learning context and the new context.

It was argued in the *Introduction* that part of the 'problem' that this book is seeking to address is that the NC is over focused on subjects and the mastery of the atoms of content within those subjects. Content is important, but it has dominated to the detriment of the overall development of pupils as learners. If that is the case, then *teaching thinking* must help subject teachers to encourage pupils to transfer their learning from the narrow confines of Romeo and Juliet, the American Civil War, coastal landforms or planning a picnic menu for 5 year olds to realms of the world beyond school.

Transfer is a contested topic. There are those who, on the basis of research evidence, argue that transfer does not occur, that there are no general thinking skills and everything must be learned in specific domains backed by the necessary knowledge base. They have a point: transfer is difficult; subject knowledge is important; and there are well documented cases of classroom learning failing to inform performance in real world contexts and vice-versa. Desforges & Ling (1998) have drawn upon constraint theory to suggest how classrooms do not encourage transfer. Constraint theory suggests that in problem solving and learning humans have a bias to simplifying the demands of the situation. Constraints are devices to highlight important information and shut out information perceived to be irrelevant, a kind of programmed blinkering, which limits the way a person thinks and behaves in particular contexts, such as subject classrooms. The result in the classroom is that pupils concentrate on producing 'neat, smudge-free writing if this is what the teacher rewards'. (Desforges & Ling, 1998 p394) Ford et al (1998) have summarised the evidence about the effect of the NC, which points to teachers and pupils focusing more on doing well in tests and exams and taking fewer risks, to the detriment of the chances of transfer.

There are, however, reasons for a more optimistic view of transfer. Firstly, the pessimistic view is based largely on the dominant forms of teaching that concentrate on content and do not encourage articulation of thought. Secondly, researchers and research students at Newcastle University have interviewed many pupils who provide convincing evidence that learning in some lessons does inform their disposition, information processing and problem solving in other contexts. Thirdly, it is hard to sustain an argument that transfer does not occur as it would mean that every problem we encounter is entirely novel.

Mayer & Wittrock (1996) recount four views of transfer:

> *'General Transfer of General Skill;*
> *Specific Transfer of Specific Behaviour;*
> *Specific Transfer of General Skill;*
> *Metacognitive Control of General and Specific Skills.'*

It is the last that they represent as the most promising, as it combines features of the other three. Thus Mayer & Wittrock argue that transfer is enhanced when students have learned general and specific processes or skills and the ability to select and monitor them. Furthermore they propose, on the basis of research evidence, that effective instruction ensures that students select relevant information, build internal connections between the information and develop external connections to other contexts and subject matter. They report a range of studies in which metacognitive ability has been linked with better performance. So, *teaching thinking* with debriefing holds out very different prospects for transfer as it changes the conditions for learning, by encouraging metacognition, the building of connections between existing understanding and new knowledge, and from there to new contexts. It also encourages pupils to think of themselves as active learners who have some control over their educational experience. Debriefing is a key to transfer.

Debriefing

We define debriefing broadly as small group or whole class discussion, undertaken after learning activities and designed to encourage pupils to explore and extend their learning. Debriefing, or some similar reflective process, would seem to be essential if pupils are to develop self-regulation and metacognitive awareness, which help provide the conditions for 'Metacognitive Control of General and Specific Skills'. We need to add that the success of debriefing may be dependent on the introduction, framing or briefing which can orientate pupils towards particular learning outcomes

Before giving guidance on debriefing, something must be said about language. Thought and language are intertwined. One view of this relationship is that thought is internalised speech. Without appropriate words it is difficult for humans to have any conceptions and ideas in a domain. If pupils are never given the opportunity to discuss how they have undertaken a task – their strategies for processing information, how they worked with others, the images that come into their head, how they planned and evaluated – then they will not develop a vocabulary to describe, monitor and regulate these processes. Transfer is likely to be highly dependent on pupils possessing a language for thinking and learning. Debriefing provides a new window on learning through introducing a language of thought.

Much of what we know about debriefing is the result of the work of four geography teachers: Liz Evans, David Kinninment, Julie McGrane and Amber Riches who researched the process with the help of a Teacher Training Agency Teacher Research Grant. For a fuller account of this work see Leat & Kinninment (2000). In summary they recommend the following points in planning for debriefing:

1 Debriefing is unlikely to be successful following a simple comprehension activity based on a textbook. You need to have done stimulating and challenging exercises like those in this book. Furthermore, it is useful to distinguish between three intentions in debriefing:

- getting pupils to give their answers/solutions and the reasons and skills behind them, which helps;
- getting pupils to explain how they have done a task, both in terms of their individual cognitive processes and in terms of group processes and giving them a language for these processes;
- helping pupils to see how these processes are or can be used elsewhere.

Linking to the point made above – about providing a language – you need to decide what words need introducing in each lesson in order to provide a language for thinking.

2 You have to make a decision, before or during a lesson, about the focus for debriefing – it is better not to have too many agendas. From here the issue becomes whether you are aiming to steer discussion in a particular direction to reach a predetermined outcome or genuinely wishing to explore and share the thinking of class members.

3 You also need to think very differently about the structure of lessons. You have to believe that the debriefing process is at least as important as the activity, if you want to develop metacognition and a different mindset on learning. Without this belief there is no motivation to make it happen. Several teachers have commented on how difficult it is to protect the time needed for debriefing (they just start and the bell goes). One possible remedy is to start debriefing short activities which come well before the end of the lesson. Another is to set a digital watch to buzz you when the debriefing should begin.

4 One of the most important tasks in planning is to develop analogies, stories and likely contexts in pupils' lives that allow and encourage pupils to make connections from the outcomes of a lesson (see 1 above). This shows that the subject can help pupils make sense of the world as they experience it, thus overcoming constraints to transfer. Mason (1994) usefully summarises some of the evidence relating to the effectiveness of analogies in fostering understanding.

5 If you are pursuing the intentions in 1 above, it can be useful to have a number of questions for pupils to think about quickly, for say three to five minutes. This gives them a chance to prepare their thoughts: they are not caught cold. These might include:

> *'What were your first ideas on this?'*
> *'Did you change your strategy or ideas as you worked?'*
> *'How would you do this differently if you did it again?'*

6 As a general rule, it is not productive to plan set sequences of questions. This can lead to a very wooden episode. Try to develop stock questions to use as circumstances require. However, practice alone can sensitise you to the most appropriate question for the moment. For opening discussion, such questions or prompts might be:

> *'Rachel, what have you come up with?'*
> *'Remember the question/task was… What do you think?'*

You then need prompts and questions to encourage pupils to expand on their answers, such as:

> *'Go on.'*
> *'Can you explain that in more detail?'*
> *'Why do you think that?'*

Further, remember not to interrupt: nodding, using your hands, or other body language to encourage continuation can be helpful in keeping them going. One can also have a range of questions to help open up discussion:

> *'Everybody else agree?'* or *'Anybody disagree?'*
> *'Did he answer the question?'*
> *'Kamal, I know you did something a bit different, can you tell everybody?'*

Where more detailed planning is done it tends to impede the debriefing because it makes it harder to respond to the flow of the discussion. The lessons need to be carefully planned, but it is important to retain the flexibility to respond to pupils' contributions. Maureen Hughes (1997) has highlighted this issue in a study of early years classrooms, where she concludes that it is difficult for pupils to think aloud and explore ideas if their questions are *'discouraged as an interruption to the pre-planned topic, or squeezed out by teachers' over dominant questions'*.

7 Watching and listening to groups before the whole class debriefing often provides important ingredients for this session. So, for example, if you overhear some good thinking from a group you can call upon that group to contribute their thoughts. You may be able to 'seed' a particular contribution by prompting a group with subtle comments or questions which nudge a particular line of reasoning. You can then draw on this investment in your debriefing. Pupils generally respond very positively when you say *'I know that you had some interesting ideas'*. Planning has to be interactive: teachers have global goals but they should be sensitive to the thinking of pupils. To this end it is really very useful to write down some of what you hear or see. Do not routinely interrupt groups by approaching them with the words *'How are you getting on?'* This disrupts their thinking.

8 The most important thing to bear in mind as you start the session is that you want the best thinking to be shared. Therefore, you have to keep asking pupils to respond to each other, to critique what has been said by others. However, this has to be done sensitively – it is not a competition to find the best: it is a collaboration.

9 One of the dilemmas you may face occurs when pupils' solutions or reasoning falls short of some predetermined plan, despite all your best efforts to push them further. The question is then whether you leave the pupils with the best solution or reasoning that they come up with, or do you superimpose your own? There is a temptation to do the latter because you are the 'font of wisdom and truth' as the teacher. If your intentions really are longer term and relate to developing their autonomy as thinkers and learners then you might well settle for their solutions. The danger in suddenly introducing your answer, like pulling a rabbit from a hat, is that you undermine their willingness to participate. You have been offering them a different contract, their honest and hard thinking in return for your acceptance of and respect for their thinking. You are in danger of breaking the contract.

Implications for Professional Development
The following are potentially powerful features of debriefing sessions:

- maintaining a high proportion of open questions which require the articulation of reasoning by pupils;
- encouraging pupils to extend and justify their answers, if necessary giving thinking time;
- encouraging pupils to evaluate each others' contributions to whole class discussion;
- providing evaluative feedback to pupils, not necessarily in the form of 'that was good/not so good', but in terms of criteria that pupils can apply to judge their own reasoning, such as 'what assumptions have you made?' or 'do you have evidence to back up your ideas?'
- using analogies, stories and everyday contexts to help pupils to understand the wider significance of their learning and encourage them to transfer it;
- drawing attention to the cognitive and social skills that the pupils have used, and encouraging distillation of good practice in relation to these skills;
- relating thinking and learning described by pupils to the important concepts or reasoning pattern in subjects;
- drawing upon what one has heard or seen during small-group work preceding the debriefing.

Conclusion
Skill and understanding in relation to debriefing develop through thoughtful practice. You must expect this process to take time. You must expect that some pupils may find it strange, difficult and even contrary to their notions of teaching. Some pupils may never be persuaded that it is a good use of time. You will make mistakes. You have to be committed to the idea and to learning from your experience, which is always made easier through learning collaboratively with colleagues.

Bibliography

Adey, P. & Shayer, M.
(1994) *Really Raising Standards*
London: Routledge

Advisory Group on Citizenship
(1998) *Education for Citizenship and the Teaching of Democracy in Schools* (Final Report)
London: Qualifications and Curriculum Authority

Arthur, J. & Phillips, R.
(2000) *Issues in History Teaching*
London: Routledge

Askew, M., Brown, M., Rhodes, V., Johnson, D. & Wiliam D.
(1997) *Effective Teachers of Numeracy*
London: Kings College

Banham, D.
(1998) 'Getting ready for the Grand Prix: learning how to build a substantiated argument in Year 7'
in *Teaching History, 92*

Black, P. & Wiliam, D.
(1998) *Inside the Black Box*
London: King's College

Blagg, N., Ballinger, M. & Lewis, R.
(1993) 'Development of Transferable Skills in Learners'
in *R & D Series, 18*
Cambridge: Employment Department

Brown, A. L.
(1987) 'Metacognition, executive control, self regulation and other more mysterious mechanism' in Weinert, Franz, Kluwe & Rainer (eds) *Metacognition, Motivation and Understanding*
London: Lawrence Erlbaum Associates

Brown, A. & Campione, J.
(1990) 'Communities of learning and thinking, or a context by any other name' in Kuhn, D. (ed)
Developmental Perspectives on Teaching and Learning Thinking Skills,
Contributions to Human Development Series
Basle: Karger

Byrom, J.
(2000) 'Why go on a pilgrimage? Using a concluding enquiry to reinforce and assess earlier learning'
in *Teaching History, 99*

Counsell, C.
(1997) *Analytical and Discursive Writing at Key Stage 3*
London: Historical Association

Counsell, C.
(2000) 'Historical knowledge and historical skills: a distracting dichotomy' in Arthur, J. & Phillips, R. (eds)
Issues in History Teaching
London: Routledge

Culpin, C. & Szuscikiewicz, P.
(1993) *The Era of the Second World War: Teacher's Guide*
Glasgow: Collins

D'Arcy, P.
(1989) *Oracy in Action: A Video-Based Training Package on Oracy in Secondary Schools*
Swindon: Wiltshire LEA

Desforges, C. & Lings, P.
(1998) 'Teaching Knowledge Application: Advances in Theoretical Conceptions and Their Professional Implications'
in *British Journal of Educational Studies*, Vol. 46, pp386-398

Dickinson, A. K. & Lee, P. J.
(1978) *History Teaching and Historical Understanding*
London: Heinemann.

Driver, R., Squires, A., Rushworth, P. & Wood-Robinson, V.
(1994) *Making Sense of Secondary Science*
London: Routledge

Dweck, C.
(1999) *Self Theories: Their Role in Motivation, Personality and Development*
New York: Psychology Press

Elliott, J.
(1991) *Action Research for Educational Change*
Milton Keynes: Open University Press

Ford, K., Clark, J., Leat, D. & Miller, J.
(2000) *An Analysis of Research Into The Impact Of The National Curriculum And The Implications For Teachers And Schools: Report Commissioned by The Schools Curriculum and Assessment Authority*
Newcastle: University of Newcastle-upon-Tyne

Ginsberg, M.
(1964) *Thirty Eight Witnesses*
New York: The New York Times Company

Hargreaves, A.
(1992) 'Foreword' in Hargreaves, A. & Fullan, M. (eds)
Understanding Teacher Development
London, Cassell

Hughes, M.
(1997) 'Teachers and other adults as talk-partners for pupils in nursery and reception classes' in *Summary of Doctoral Thesis Findings*
London: Teacher Training Agency

Kolb, D.
(1984) *Experiential Learning*
New Jersey: Prentice Hall

Kruger, A.C.
(1993) 'Peer collaboration: conflict, cooperation or both?'
in *Social Development*, Vol. 2, pp165-182

Leat, D.
(1998) *Thinking Through Geography*
Cambridge: Chris Kington Publishing

Leat, D.
(1999) 'Rolling the Stone Uphill: teacher development and the implementation of Thinking Skills programmes'
in *Oxford Review of Education*, Vol. 25, pp387-403

Leat, D. & Kinninment, D.
(2000) 'Learn to Debrief' in Fisher, C. & Binns T. (eds)
Issues in Geography Teaching
London: Routledge Falmer

Leat, D. & Nichols, A.
(1999) *Mysteries Make You Think*
Sheffield: Geographical Association

Light, P. & Butterworth G. (eds)
(1992) *Context and Cognition: Ways of Learning and Knowing*
London: Harvester Wheatsheaf

Mason, L.
(1994) Analogy, Metaconceptual Awareness and Conceptual Change: a classroom study
in *Educational Studies*, Vol. 20 pp. 267-291

Mayer, R. & Wittrock, M.
(1996) Problem-Solving Transfer in Berliner, D. & Calfee, R. (eds) *Handbook of Educational Psychology*
New York: Simon & Schuster Macmillan

Nichol, J.
(1995) *Teaching History at Key Stage 3*
Cambridge: Chris Kington Publishing

Norman, K. (ed)
(1992) *Thinking Voices: The Work of the National Oracy Project*
London: Hodder & Stoughton

Perkins, D. & Salomon, G.
(1988) Teaching for Transfer
Educational Leadership, Vol. 46, pp22-32

Riley, C.
(1999) 'Evidential understanding, period knowledge and the development of literacy: a practical approach to 'layers of inference' for Key Stage 3'
in *Teaching History*, 97

Riley, M.
(2000) 'Into the KS3 History Garden: Choosing and planting your enquiry questions'
in *Teaching History*, 99

Sarason, S.
(1982) *The Culture of the School and the Problem of Change*
Boston: Allyn & Bacon

Schemitt, D.
(1980) *Evaluation Study: Schools Council History Project*
Glasgow: Holmes McDougall

Schools Curriculum and Assessment Authority
(1997) *Extended Writing in KS3 History*
London: SCAA

Schools Council History Project
(1972) *History 13-16 Project*
Glasgow: Holmes McDougall

Sharan, S.
(1980) 'Cooperative Learning in Small Groups: Recent methods and effects on achievement, attitudes and ethnic relations'
in *Review of Educational Research*, Vol. 50, pp241-247

Shephard, C., Corbishley, M. & Large, A.
(1995) *Contrast and Connections*
London: John Murray

Sinclair, J. & Coulthard, M.
(1975) *Towards an Analysis of Discourse: the Language of Teachers and Pupils*
London: Oxford University Press

Smith, A.
Accelerated Learning in the Classroom
Stafford: Network Educational Press

Stanford, G.
(1990) *Developing Effective Classroom Groups*
Bristol: Acora Books

Teaching History
(2000) 'Defining Progression'
edition *Teaching History*, 98

Further useful reading

Unstead, R.
(1956) *Teaching History in the Junior School*
London: A & C Black

von Wright, J.
(1992) 'Reflections on Learning'
in *Learning and Instruction, Vol. 2*, pp59-68

Wood, D.
(1980) 'Teaching the Young Child: Some
relationships between social interaction, language
and thought' in Olson D. (ed) The *Social
Foundations of Language and Thought*
New York: Norton

Wrenn, A.
(1999) 'Build it in: don't bolt it on: history's
opportunity to support critical citizenship' in
Teaching History, 97

Baron, J.B. & Sternberg, R.J.
(1987) *Teaching Thinking Skills: Theory and Practice*
New York: Freeman

Maclure, S. & Davies, P.
(1991) *Learning to Think: Thinking to Learn - The
Proceedings of the 1989 OECD Conference*
Oxford: Pergamon Press

McGuinness, C.
(1999) *From Thinking Skills to Thinking Classrooms: a
review and evaluation of approaches for developing pupils'
thinking.* DfEE Research Report RR115
London: Department for Education and Employment

Mercer, N.
(2000) *Words and Minds: How we use Language to Think
Together*
London: Routledge

Nickerson, R.S., Perkins, D.N. & Smith, E.E.
(1985) *The Teaching of Thinking*
New Jersey: Lawrence Erlbaum Associates

Wood, D.
(1988) *How Children Think and Learn*
Oxford: Blackwell